Focus

'The medium of film has increasing power in the postmodern world. In this highly readable and accessible book, Tony Watkins rightly urges us to respond to our "movie-made culture" with God-directed wisdom.'

Jeremy Begbie, Vice-Principal, Ridley Hall, Cambridge

'In an age where film and media is the dominant language of the times, we need able, clear, Christian, insightful voices to offer guidance for those seeking to live well. I heartily recommend this book as a vital resource for an informed Christian journey.'

Stuart McAllister, International Director, Ravi Zacharias International Ministries

'You've seen the films – now read the book. *Focus: the Art and Soul of Cinema* is an engaging, thoughtful and challenging study, but be warned, after reading this you may never watch a movie in the same way again!'

Chris Stoddard, Reaching the Unchurched Network

'This is an extremely insightful guide to the movies. It will help anyone engage thoughtfully with what films are trying to say in our contemporary culture. Covering a wide range of film, classic and modern, Tony Watkins demonstrates the importance of understanding the worldviews that have influenced them. I highly recommend reading this book before your next trip to the multiplex!'

Chris Sinkinson, Pastor and Lecturer in Apologetics at Moorlands College, Bournemouth

'Focus is a breath of fresh air – an enthusiastic, thorough and profoundly practical exploration of the relationship between films and worldviews. Anyone who wants to engage with

films from a Christian perspective will be helped immeasurably in this careful, comprehensive and insightful book.'
Lars Dahle, Academic Dean, Gimlekollen School of Journalism and Communication, Norway

'I still vividly remember, though it was 20 years ago, watching a film with a group of students and then leading a discussion on what it was trying to communicate. My opening questions were greeted with blank stares. After an awkward silence, brave souls started to contribute their embryonic thoughts. The problem? They were watching the film in 'entertainment mode' rather than thoughtfully engaging with its message.

I am delighted that Tony Watkins has written the book that those students needed 20 years ago! For all of us who enjoy films this book will help us think more deeply about how to watch thoughtfully and critique using biblical principles. Tony knows the Bible and he knows the world of film. This is a great book!'
Elaine Duncan, Chief Executive of the Scottish Bible Society

'All of us know the influence of film in contemporary society but we often lack the necessary equipment to both understand and engage with the medium. With no reliable compass, Christians can often stray into the territories of Irrational Avoidance, Dangerous Assimilation or Embarrassing "Christianising". Tony Watkins knows about films and film-making, but more importantly he has developed an all-encompassing Christian worldview through which he can faithfully analyse the medium. In this book, he gives us a map of biblical reality that will enable Christians to penetrate deeply into the Art and Soul of Cinema. For our own holiness, for those we seek to evangelise, and for Christ's lordship over all of culture (including film) this book is a welcome help and guide.'
Daniel Strange, Lecturer in Culture, Religion and Public Theology, Oak Hill Theological College, London

'Film is a powerful influence in modern life. This intelligent book helps us understand the world of film better. More, it gives us useable tools to relate creatively and critically to what is going on before our very eyes. Tony Watkins is deeply rooted in Christian thinking and up to date in the world of film. An important book!'

Stefan Gustavsson, Director, Credo Academy and General Secretary, Swedish Evangelical Alliance

'Nothing shapes the imagination of this generation more than the movies. There is no better channel for engaging with the ideas of the culture or a more pressing area for Christian discernment. Tony Watkins has produced an excellent introduction to the whole subject – comprehensive, balanced, readable and immanently useful. *Focus: The Art and Soul of Cinema* will help orient you to both the opportunities and the challenges of our media-saturated culture.'

Jock McGregor, L'Abri Fellowship

Focus

The Art and Soul of Cinema

Tony Watkins

www.DamarisBooks.com

Authentic

LONDON • ATLANTA • HYDERABAD

First published in 2007 by Damaris Books,
an imprint of Authentic Media
9 Holdom Avenue, Bletchley, Milton Keynes, Bucks, MK1 1QR, UK
285 Lynnwood Avenue, Tyrone, GA 30290, USA
OM Authentic Media, Medchal Road, Jeedimetla Village,
Secunderabad 500 055, A. P.
www.authenticmedia.co.uk
Authentic Media is a division of Send the Light Ltd.,
a company limited by guarantee (registered charity no. 270162)

British Library Cataloguing in Publication Data

A catalogue record for this book is available from the British Library.

978-1-904753-15-5

Typeset in 11/13 Palatino

Cover Design by fourninezero design.
Printed in Great Britain by Print on Demand Worldwide

For Jane, the love of my life, who endured my preoccupation with the long process of research and writing. Film-watching – along with everything else – is always best when I share it with you.

Contents

Acknowledgements

In any book of this sort there has to be the equivalent of a speech at the Oscars – and this is the closest I'll probably ever get. There are many people to whom I owe my sincere thanks for giving me input and direction which has finally brought me to the point of writing this book. I cannot possibly mention them all, but a few people over the years particularly stand out. In many ways, this book is a direct consequence of Richard Perry persuading me to start reading Francis Schaeffer's work while I was a student – a small action with enormous consequences. I am so grateful to him for starting me down this track and encouraging me along the way for over twenty years. My time on the staff of the Universities and Colleges Christian Fellowship provided many opportunities to have my thinking enriched by a large number of people, both staff and others. In the areas covered by this book, I am especially grateful for what I learned from Bob Horn, David Cook, Don Carson and Jim Sire during this period.

Since then, the Damaris team has been a constant source of stimulation and encouragement and I'm thankful to all of them. I must make particular mention of Nick Pollard with whom it has been a privilege to work since 1996. The members of the first Damaris Study Group[1] in Southampton also deserve special thanks. I'm grateful, too, for the many groups who have allowed me to teach some of the material which has ultimately grown into this book, whether in workshops or lectures. So many individuals in these situations have stimulated, stretched and challenged my thinking on these issues. I am particularly grateful for the opportunities to teach some of it at the Keswick Convention, Agape's summer staff conference in 2005 and especially at the Gimlekollen School of Journalism and Communication in Norway.

There are a number of people who have been very helpful during the actual writing of the book, and I'm deeply grateful to them all. Members of the Arts and Faith discussion forum[2] have enriched my thinking on films with their insightful perspectives and vigorous debates. Damaris Intern Emily Dalrymple kept up the flow of material for CultureWatch enabling me to stay more focused on writing this book. Rich Cline, Lars and Margunn Dahle, Caroline Puntis, Brittany Waggoner and Joel Wilson all made extremely helpful and insightful comments on the manuscript. Di Archer copy-edited the manuscript and Steve Couch valiantly attempted to steer me through the process on time, giving much valuable input and feedback along the way. However, more than anyone, it is my family – my wife Jane, and sons Charlie, Oliver and Pip – to whom I am immeasurably grateful for their patience, encouragement and love.

Tony Watkins, October 2006

Notes

1 Damaris Study Groups are now known as CultureWatch Groups.
2 www.artsandfaith.com.

Introduction

People love films. Whether it is going out for an evening at the cinema with a box of popcorn, or curling up at home with a DVD and a bar of chocolate, movies are one of our favourite forms of entertainment. They make us laugh and cry; they thrill us and scare us; they transport us to faraway places and bring to life things that we could only dream of; they stretch our thinking and enable us to see life through different eyes.

In the eighties, though, many people were predicting the death of cinema – as happened in the 1950s when television first became common. The fear in the movie industry was that people would no longer go out for this kind of entertainment. By the eighties, television had become a core part of life for the vast majority of people in the western world, and home video was taking off in a big way. We could watch films at home whenever we wanted – so why go to the cinema? Cinemas across Britain and other western countries – particularly in smaller towns, and the outskirts of larger population centres – shut their doors for the last time.

It is clear now, however, that the obituaries for cinema were very premature. There was still an appetite for the experience of watching a film on the big screen with the lights down. But some aspects of the experience had to change. To woo punters back, film exhibitors needed to transform the old flea pits and find ways of operating cinemas economically. And so the multiplex was born – a smart complex of smaller auditoria with the latest sound and projection equipment. It all adds up to a rather different experience than in the days of single-screen theatres, but film is once again big business and people love movies as much as ever.

We still love going to the cinema – a central aspect of which, for most people, is being with friends and talking about the film afterwards – and we love watching them at home. The advent of DVDs has created a revolution in our viewing – more than VHS ever did. A key factor is the new possibilities that come with DVD. Extras such as commentary tracks, behind-the-scenes features and deleted scenes allow us to find out more than we ever could about the story behind the story and how the film was constructed. DVDs also make possible a perfect freeze frame – something that even the best VHS machines could not achieve. As Laura Mulvey argues, the ability to study an individual frame in a film or to watch sections of the film in slow motion enables us to engage with the film in new ways.[1] A further revolution is now under way, with downloading of movies from the Internet becoming a reality. It almost certainly means that the days of DVD are numbered. I do not know what the implications for cinemas will be, but I am sure our love affair with film means that we will still want the excitement of going out and experiencing movies on a big screen.

With a revival of cinema-going, new technologies transforming our engagement with films, and new television channels enabling us both to see more films and to find out more about them,[2] our culture is becoming increasingly film-literate.[3] It is therefore more important than ever before that Christians should understand the significance of films within our culture and be able to engage with them. Film is a wonderfully rich medium. We see a rapid succession of moving images – in a cinema we see them on a huge scale. The images are accompanied by dialogue, sound effects and a musical score. All these elements combine to create meaning – to tell a story that may resonate with our own experience, or perhaps move us or make us laugh, excite us or scare us. Gordon Matties writes:

> Because it works at so many levels, film can have insidious power or extravagant grace. For this reason film invites critical reflection on experience. It offers a wonderful opportunity to bring experience, analysis, emotion and action together. Film is 'kinaesthetic' in that it involves our whole being. Film therefore creates a context for discernment that is holistic – theologically, ethically, and spiritually.[4]

It is important for our ongoing Christian growth that we learn to watch films thoughtfully rather than let them wash over us, seeing them as mere entertainment. It is important for our ability to relate to our friends that we learn to understand the messages which films communicate and how they relate to the good news of Jesus Christ.

So this is a book about understanding films. We will consider how films communicate their messages and how we can engage with them, digging beneath the surface to think about beliefs and values. It can seem like a formidable challenge at first, but as with everything it gets easier the more practice you get. A number of people over the years have suggested that it rather spoils our entertainment to be thinking critically at the same time. I don't think so – at least, in the longer term. In the short term, while getting used to thinking about films in this way, it may feel more like hard work than enjoyment. But as one becomes familiar with this way of thinking, it begins to be second nature, an integral part of watching a movie. In fact, rather than diminish our pleasure, I would argue that before too long it positively enhances it.

As I have said already, film is an immensely rich audio-visual medium and film-makers put a great deal of effort into their work. So we will be rewarded for paying closer attention to what we see and hear. We will spot more of the connections – both between one part of the film and another, and between one particular film and other films, books and other aspects of culture. We will discover deeper levels of meaning and understand more fully what the film-maker wanted to communicate – as well as that which he or she communicated unwittingly (as Federico Fellini once remarked, 'Even if I set out to make a film about a fillet of sole, it would be about me'[5]). My experience is that this is an altogether richer encounter with a film, and one which thus deepens and extends my enjoyment. It is just the same with all other arts – the more we understand, the more we gain from each experience.

I also want to respond to the 'thinking too hard spoils my enjoyment' suggestion by asking, 'So what if it does?' Like the men of Issachar who 'understood the times and knew what Israel should do',[6] we need to understand our context and, as we will see, movies are a very important and powerful window into the worldviews that surround us. Even if our enjoyment of movies – or books or television – is lessened by approaching it in such a way that I understand my world better, I should do it anyway. Since when has my personal entertainment and enjoyment been the key criterion in deciding when and how to live for the kingdom?

The suggestion that Christians should not or need not think too hard is deeply revealing. Peter Fraser characterises American Christians (but equally true of many Christians in other countries): 'We . . . are led by cultural convention and undeveloped tastes and judgment to embrace the idols of the crowd.'[7] He points out that the problem faced by the church is not so much the films which are around, but 'our collective lack of judgment produced by a lack of training. We don't know how to measure and evaluate film from a Christian point of view. We hardly know what a Christian point of view is toward art . . .'[8] Later, Fraser declares that, 'the time is at hand for Christians to engage our movie-made culture courageously, and this means we have to struggle with tough issues and tell the truth . . . When we stand back from engaging the world, in this case, the world of film, and instead allow ourselves to be treated like village idiots, we can hardly expect God to be pleased.'[9] So we should watch movies for understanding more than for entertainment. However, the process of doing so is in itself far more enjoyable than merely sitting back and letting it all wash over me. And it gives us much more to talk about afterwards – hopefully in intelligent, stimulating and engaging ways.

First, though, we need to consider cinema in a much wider context. The first section of this book (the First Reel) is the set-up, providing the context for everything that follows. Chapter 1 is an establishing shot – a wide-angle view which sets the scene and introduces the two opposing forces at work. In this chapter I set out the theological foundation on which my engagement with film is based: a biblical understanding of culture. In Chapter 2, I cut to a different scene to pick out some important themes that will keep recurring as I consider the implications of this view of culture for how we think about movies. This chapter is an introduction to analysing worldviews since, 'Movies do not merely portray a world; they propagate a worldview.'[10] All films communicate worldviews, so Chapter 3 is a flashback, explaining something of the influence of worldviews on cinema since its earliest days. These worldviews continue to influence and shape what we see on our screens today. There are many worldviews which I could have addressed, especially if I was taking world cinema into account. But in a book of this size, I needed to limit myself, so I have focused on four key worldviews and their influence on the development of western cinema – the tradition which still dominates globally.

In the Second Reel, we get down to the nitty-gritty of the subject. Chapter 4 gives us some close-ups of film-making, looking at who makes movies and how they communicate their messages through cinematic techniques. Chapter 5 is also close in, focusing on how the stories within films are constructed. Chapter 6 zooms out a little to reflect on how film genres are related to worldviews. The Third Reel of the book is the climax. Chapter 7 is a tracking shot which enables us to draw together some of the strands and highlight some of the key messages which movies communicate. Finally, we reach the resolution as we turn our attention to ourselves and focus on how we respond to films – and help others to do so. The 'extras', as it were, comprise a pair of appendices: the first is a series of questions which I find useful as I engage with films; the second considers the issue of sex and violence in films. There are more extras, and some useful links, online at www.damaris. org/focus/.

Before we start I need to warn you that there are some big spoilers in this book. I refer to over 300 films and do not give away the plot twists or endings for the vast majority of them. But there are some examples which it was impossible to discuss and make important points about without letting some cats out of the bag. This is a book to help you understand what films are really saying, and then to engage with those ideas. My hope is that, after reading this book, the process of watching a film will be even more fun than it was before, and that as you develop more insight into films, your conversations about them will be more stimulating than ever.

Notes

1 Laura Mulvey, *Death 24X a Second: Stillness and the Moving Image* (London: Reaktion Books, 2005).
2 'Eat Cinema', for example, is a UK channel devoted to film and designed to promote cinema-going.
3 James Monaco proposed the term 'cinemate' in *How to Read a Film: Movies, Media, Multimedia*, third edition (New York and Oxford: Oxford University Press, 2000) p. 152.
4 Gordon Matties, 'What do movies do?' – www.cmu.ca/faculty/gmatties/What%20do%20movies%20do.htm.
5 *The Atlantic*, December 1965, quoted on www.wikiquote.org/wiki/Federico_Fellini.
6 1 Chronicles 12:32.
7 Peter Fraser and Vernon Edwin Neal, *ReViewing the Movies: A Christian Response to Contemporary Film* (Wheaton, Ill.:

     Crossway, 2000) p. 11.

 8 Fraser and Neal, *ReViewing the Movies*, p. 12.

 9 Fraser and Neal, *ReViewing the Movies*, p. 20.

10 Bryan P. Stone, *Faith and Film: Theological Themes at the Cinema* (St. Louis, Mo.: Chalice Press, 2000) p. 6.

First Reel:
Worldviews and Films

1. Cinema Paradiso

Film and Culture

Truman Burbank (Jim Carrey) lives a pleasant, quiet life in the picture-perfect island town of Seahaven. Yet beneath the untroubled surface of his existence run currents of dissatisfaction and fear. Truman and his wife Meryl (Laura Linney) do not really love each other. His heart still belongs to Lauren (Natascha McElhone), the girl with whom he fell in love at college but who was promptly whisked away by her father. Ever since, Truman has longed to escape the tranquil but empty world of Seahaven and find his way to Fiji where he was told Lauren was going. He is held back by his fear: he has been terrified of water since his father was washed off their boat and drowned in a storm when Truman was a boy.

What Truman does not know is that virtually his entire life is a sham. He has lived since birth in a gigantic television studio. Everyone in his life is an actor: Truman alone is genuine (hence his name) in the way he relates to others. The love between Truman and Lauren had been real too, albeit momentary. As soon as they had fallen for each other, she had tried to explain what was really going on and so was abruptly torn away from him. The perfect appearance of the simulated reality in which Truman lives is contrasted with a hopelessly imperfect image of his true love. In his basement he conceals a picture made up of parts of various faces which he has torn from magazines in a desperate attempt to build up an image of Lauren.

One day some bizarre incidents intensify Truman's feeling that all is not right with the world, as well as his longing to be reunited with Lauren. He cannot hold back any longer and tries to leave Seahaven, but every attempt is thwarted: there are no flights available, the bus has broken down, the ferry has no captain, and an accident at the nearby nuclear power station prevents him driving away. Everyone and everything seem to be conspiring to stop him leaving. His only option is to face his fear and take to the water again. Under cover of darkness he slips away in a sailing boat only to find a huge storm blowing up with lightning repeatedly striking the mast of the boat. Is even the weather trying to stop him? Truman clings to the mast and rages: 'Is that the best you can do? You're going to have to kill me!'

God is in the Details

It is easy to forget that we, the viewers of *The Truman Show* (Peter Weir, 1998), are effectively omniscient: we know why these things are happening to Truman, whereas he has no idea. We know about Christof (Ed Harris), the director of the television show, and the way he controls Truman's life, manipulating actors and events and even the weather. When Truman is shouting at the storm we might automatically assume that he is addressing Christof, but in fact he has no inkling whatsoever of Christof's existence or that he lives in a TV studio. He can only be railing at God himself. Christof is, of course, in the place of God in Truman's life: he had filmed Truman before he was even born, had him adopted at birth and dictated the entire course of his life. He even apparently has power of life and death over Truman, summoning up a tidal wave that threatens to engulf the boat and drown the star of his show.

Truman is not drowned, however, and the storm abates. He sails on with the sun on his face and the wind in the air. He is heading towards freedom – when suddenly the boat crashes to a stop. The blue sky and distant horizon turn out to be a wall. What would that experience do to someone's view of reality? Truman beats his arms against the wall in despair before finally stepping off the boat. A tracking shot follows Truman walking along by the wall, apparently on the surface of the water, and ascending some stairs[1] where he finds a door marked Exit. As he reaches out to the handle, a voice speaks from the cloud. 'Who are you?' asks Truman. Even now, could Truman really imagine that this is a TV director addressing him rather than God? Christof speaks, telling Truman (with a perfectly-timed mid-sentence pause) that he is 'the creator – of a television show'. Christof explains Truman's situation and uses God-like language to persuade him that he should not leave ('I've seen you your whole life . . .').

On the sail of Truman's boat is the number 139.[2] Why? Try reading Psalm 139 while watching Truman's escape and see what (negative) resonance these lines have in that context:

Where can I go from your Spirit?
Where can I flee from your presence
If I go up to the heavens, you are there;
if I make my bed in the depths,[3] you are there.
If I rise on the wings of the dawn,
if I settle on the far side of the sea,
even there your hand will guide me,
your right hand will hold me fast.
If I say, 'Surely the darkness will hide me
and the light become night around me,'
even the darkness will not be dark to you;
the night will shine like the day,[4]
for darkness is as light to you.[5]

The psalm praises God for his intimate knowledge of us and his care for us which has no limits. Christof's knowledge and control is not, however, presented in a positive way; rather he is seen to be a manipulative tyrant who serves his own ends by keeping Truman imprisoned in his simplistic world. He finally says to Truman, 'There's no more truth out there than there is in the world I created for you. The same lies; the same deceits. Only in my world, you have nothing to fear.' But Truman is taking charge of his own destiny and is throwing off the shackles of this quasi-God.[6] He opens the door and steps into complete blackness. For me, it is one of the most powerful images in any film. Truman has absolutely no idea about what the real world on the other side is like, but that way lies freedom.

Discerning Viewers

How do people respond to this film when they watch it? Audiences are very diverse, and every viewer brings their own likes, dislikes, interests and perspectives to their encounter with the film. Some enjoy a well-written story and what seems like a happy ending without giving it much thought. They are like the viewers of Truman's television show right at the very end of the film who, after the drama of his escape, ask what is on the other channels. More reflective viewers might see that it contains a powerful critique of our media-saturated society. Careful attention reveals the film's anti-religious theme: some viewers celebrate its suggestion that we should embrace freedom by taking charge of our own destinies, and throwing off the shackles of the idea of God. Some Christians also pick up this sentiment and condemn the film and its message as a result, while others see it more as a critique of oppressive, authoritarian religion rather than of God himself or of true faith.

It is clear that the most significant messages of the film are discerned not by casual, thoughtless viewing, but by giving careful consideration to it. It is the same with any movie. Although it is true that few people think about films in such depth, if we want to engage with them – and with our friends who watch them – we need to. We must learn to see and hear what the film-makers are trying to communicate, and the better we can do so, the more effectively we can engage with our culture. I believe we have a responsibility to do this since we are called to love God with all our minds, as well as every other aspect of our beings, and we are called to love our neighbour as ourselves.[7] If we really want to love our neighbours, then I believe that we need to understand the culture in which we live alongside each other and which exerts such enormous influence on us all.

What is Culture?

Before we get into the detail of how to understand films, however, we need to consider a broader question: what is culture? It does not mean the world of fine art, classical music, theatre and literature, though all of these are part of it. These are things I love deeply, but to think of culture only in these terms is far too narrow and elitist. A broader understanding is to see culture as a particular society at a particular time. So we might talk about the Aztec culture in Central America between the fourteenth and sixteenth centuries. Culture can mean the knowledge, values, attitudes and practices that are shared by a society, or of a group within a society. UNESCO says that culture

> should be regarded as the set of distinctive spiritual, material, intellectual and emotional features of society or a social group, and that it encompasses, in addition to art and literature, lifestyles, ways of living together, value systems, traditions and beliefs.[8]

There are a number of important components to this definition: culture involves communities; it includes both external expressions (art, literature, ways of living together, traditions) and internal aspects (value systems and beliefs). So perhaps we could distil a simpler definition of culture: the ways people in communities view, and respond to, themselves and their world.

A World Reflecting its Creator

It is interesting to compare this with the biblical account of God's creation in the first two chapters of Genesis. We learn that the creation is orderly (1:14–19) and under-standable (2:19–20); it has both functional (1:29–30; 2:9) and aesthetic aspects (2:9,12); there is an interdependence to creation (1:29; 2:15) and it has a moral dimension (1:28). Human beings are created as the pinnacle of God's creation, uniquely made in his image (1:26).

We need to consider what we mean by the 'image of God'. The primary meaning of the phrase is about humanity being God's *representative* rather than being a *representation* of God. This is seen in the command to rule in God's place, on his behalf in verse 26.[9] But this verse also uses a second word – 'likeness' – to stress that we also reflect some of the characteristics of God. In what ways are we like God? We are rational beings, able to think, anticipate and plan. We are relational beings, made to communicate and to give and receive love just as God does within the persons of the Trinity. We are creative beings with an aesthetic appreciation. We can fashion things out of the raw materials around us and declare them, in some measure, to be good. We are moral beings created to do what is right. There are other characteristics we could mention, but the most important of all is that we are spiritual beings. We may share our physicality with the animals, but we are made to transcend that in a spiritual relationship with God himself. Since we are created beings, we only possess these qualities to a limited degree, but nevertheless we are like God and bear his image.

Humanity's role in creation is evident in Genesis 1–2 with specific responsibilities either explicitly stated or implied. We are to rule on God's behalf (1:26) and be fruitful (1:28); we are to work, which encompasses caring for the environment (2:15); we are to investigate and develop the world around us (1:15; 2:19–20); ultimately

we are to obey God. This obedience points to the relationship between God and human beings, but this is not the
only relationship, of course. There is a relationship
between humanity and the environment, with us being
responsible for its well-being at some level.[10] The climax
of Genesis 2 is the relationship between the man and
woman – a relationship so profound that throughout the
Bible it is used as a picture of God's relationship with his
people. Relationships within the wider family and
community are implied by the command to, 'Be fruitful
and increase in number; fill the earth' (1:28), although it is
not until Genesis 4:17 that we see this in action.[11]

These explicit or implicit instructions to human beings
before the Fall are known as the 'cultural mandate'. As
Nancy Pearcey writes, 'it tells us that our original
purpose was to create cultures, build civilizations –
nothing less.'[12] It gives us a biblical framework for what
culture should be: people living in communities, expressing their creativity, and investigating and developing
their world. This is, essentially, a different way of
expressing my previous simple definition of culture as
'the ways people in communities view, and respond to,
themselves and their world'. The implication of this
understanding of culture is enormous: it means that
culture is God's idea. It is something which arises out of
God's goodness in creation. It should, therefore, never be
understood by Christians as being irredeemably hostile
to Christian faith. It means that we should be very excited
about culture, involved in it and working to transform
and redeem it.

A World Resisting its Creator

However, as we know only too well, there is a flip side. Culture is dangerous since it is also bound up with our rebellion against God as we see in Genesis 3. The serpent starts (v. 1) by introducing a note of scepticism about God: 'Did God *really* say . . .?' He misquotes God's command,[13] planting a seed of doubt in the woman's mind. She responds to his question but goes too far, adding 'and we must not even touch it' (v. 3).[14] The snake moves on to a flat denial of what God had said – 'You will not certainly die!' (v. 4) – before misrepresenting God and his motivations: 'For God knows that when you eat of it, your eyes will be opened and you will be like God, knowing good and evil' (v. 5). The snake makes Eve begin to feel that God does not have humanity's best interests at heart, that God is keeping back from them something that is good – something that should rightfully be theirs. So she takes the fruit and eats it.

The deep desire of Eve's heart is not so much to eat this particular fruit. Rather it is to be like God. It is, in fact, a legitimate desire – up to a point. It *should* be the deepest desire of our hearts to become more and more like the one who created us. But it is a desire that the tempter has twisted and exploited. Eve has been seduced by the possibility of becoming like God in the wrong way, a way that is entirely inappropriate for finite, created human beings. Eve wants wisdom – but God has endowed her and Adam with all the wisdom they need to rule in his place and to investigate and develop their world. She wants different wisdom, though: wisdom to know good and evil. Eve craves freedom – but they already have immense freedom, with just the one restriction on eating from the tree of the knowledge of good and evil. She

wants *absolute* freedom: freedom to make her own rules
for her life. In other words, Eve wants to be autonomous
– literally 'a law unto oneself'.

The essence of disobeying God is making my own
choices about right and wrong; making myself the centre
of my world. In other words, I take on God's role for
myself. Don Carson's memorable phrase for this is 'the
de-godding of God'.[15] It is idolatry. There is no more
fundamental sin that we can commit than to deny God's
rule and nature. There is no more serious rebellion
against God than to usurp his role for ourselves – to
become idolaters, worshipping ourselves, in effect.[16] The
details of how we express our rebellion are, at one level,
neither here nor there. Once I have dared to think that I
can be God, choosing for myself what I can or cannot do,
the ultimate sin has become part of me.

So human beings have to face serious consequences
which are experienced at a number of different levels.
First, every aspect of God's image within human beings
is damaged or broken. We remain spiritual beings, but
the spiritual part of us is so badly broken that Paul
declares it to be dead.[17] Our spiritual nature longs for
fulfilment, it longs to be alive again, but it cannot make
itself so. Our relationships become damaged and twisted.
Rather than being based on openness and intimacy (the
significance of nudity in Genesis 2:25), we see that they
are now characterised by shame, blame, oppression and
exploitation (e.g. 3:10,12,16). Our creativity becomes
corrupted, so that instead of producing only sublimely
beautiful art, we also produce pornography. Our
relationship with the environment becomes corrupted, so
that instead of having a beautiful world in which
humanity and nature live in a delicate, mutual interdependence and harmonious balance, we have an

environmental crisis on our hands. Work, instead of being something that is a pure joy – as it would have been before the Fall – now becomes difficult and a drudge, sometimes even a torment. We also have to face a real, objective guilt, and a subjective sense of shame. We are on the receiving end of God's anger, and rightly so because we have rebelled against the creator of the universe, against the fabric of reality, against the one whose very nature defines the good.

These consequences are incredibly serious, and they are apparent within culture. Culture as God intended it should be wonderful, but we have to acknowledge that the reality we experience is often awful because it is disconnected from God. Culture is comprised of fractured communities; it is people misusing their creativity; it is people exploiting their world. The cultural mandate still stands, but now everything about it is more difficult.

Reality Bites

If we want to understand our culture, and the films through which people express themselves, we have to allow for both of these faces of reality. On the one hand, culture is fabulous because it is invented by God and the product of human beings who bear God's likeness. On the other hand, culture is terrible because it is also the expression of human rebellion against God. This is true of everything that we experience in our cultural worlds. Every culture has both fantastic things that reflect God, and appalling things that reflect our disobedience. Every individual has aspects within them that are like God and aspects that are entirely unlike him. I will not be finally rid of my sinful human nature until the new heavens and new earth, but someone who is not a Christian cannot ever be entirely free of bearing God's image. It is how we are made by God, and there is no hint in the Bible that humans ceased to be so after the Fall. Indeed, Genesis 9:6 seems to reaffirm that humans continue as God's image bearers after the flood. James makes no distinction between Christians and others when he laments our use of the tongue to curse 'those who have been made in the image of God'.[18]

This two-faced nature of human beings profoundly affects our creative activity. Whether a film is written by Christians or not, it will inevitably display something of both our human glory and our shame, though the balance of these two characteristics will vary.[19] There is good and bad about everything and in everyone. Woody Allen may deny the existence of God and stress the absurdity of the universe, yet his creativity, his restless curiosity about the big questions of life, and his explorations of the complexities of relationships are evidence that he still bears something of the image of God. Quentin Tarantino may produce incredibly violent films, but *Pulp Fiction* (1994) is a significant exploration of the concept of grace. Stanley Kubrick's final film, *Eyes Wide Shut* (1999), is a story about a man's dangerous sexual adventures after his wife confesses to having once contemplated an affair. Kubrick apparently wanted to show the destructive consequences of decadence and infidelity. If this is true, he was right to try to reinforce the value of marriage and the importance of sexual relationships being kept to that context alone. But to linger over the decadence and infidelity ends up making it attractive to viewers, and this is a distortion of something wonderful and God-given. Our sexual urges may express themselves in sinful ways but the basic desire is part of how God made us. The issue about violence and sex in films is an important one, but is not central to the flow of this book and has been discussed by many other writers.[20] I therefore discuss it briefly in Appendix 2.

It is absolutely vital that we keep in mind that every person is a rebellious image-bearer (or an image-bearing rebel) and every culture is the product of rebellious image-bearers. So as we engage with communities, and with the ways in which people have investigated and developed their world and expressed their creativity, we must contend with all the contradictions and tensions which go with this two-faced reality.

Walk the Line

This rich, balanced understanding of culture is vital if we are to engage with films fully. Otherwise we will fall into one of two traps – escapism or conformism. Christians have always tended to fall into one of these two opposite pitfalls. On the one side is the response which sees culture as worldly, godless and contaminating. We should, therefore, be different and separate from it. We should maintain our holiness and not go where non-Christians go, nor do what they do, nor watch what they watch. But this is escapism. It is exemplified by the Pharisees[21] who strongly objected to Jesus mixing with those they considered to be the low-life of society. It leads to a situation where we have no meaningful relationships with those outside the church – and good relationships are vital if we are to communicate the good news of Jesus Christ through actions and words. The less connected

with our culture we are, the more difficult we will find it
to be salt and light.[22]

The other trap is a reaction to the first, saying that we
should be in the world, completely identifying with it.
We should be like everyone else, going to the same places
and doing the same things. We should be indistinguish-
able from those who are not Christians so as to not
alienate them. It is all too easy to end up conforming to
the world's standards and patterns. Taking them all on
board uncritically leads to us losing our distinctiveness as
Christians – or worse, as happened with Demas who
deserted Paul because he 'loved this world'.[23] If we have
conformed to the world we may have great relationships
with friends who are not Christians, but our ability to
communicate the good news of Jesus Christ is drastically
compromised. We become salt that has lost its saltiness.[24]

There is some truth in both of these perspectives, but
they both go too far. We should neither be over-critical of
culture nor uncritical. Somehow we have to walk a
middle path – a tightrope – between the two traps,
balancing the two biblical requirements to engage with
our culture and to grow in holiness. Neither of these is
optional. It is hard to stay balanced, however, and Jesus –
who exemplified doing so in his incarnation – knows it.
His prayer in John 17 is, among other things, for us to
stay on the tightrope. Jesus talks about the fact that we
are in the world (v. 11), and he is not praying for the
Father to remove us from it but for him to protect us. At
the same time we are not of the world (v. 14); we are
different from it. When push comes to shove we should
fall on the side of maintaining our holiness at the expense
of engagement. We can easily re-engage with the culture
at a later time. If we fall on the side of engaging with
culture at the expense of holiness, we may compromise

ourselves in some way and end up damaging our Christian lives. In the kind of world that we live in, it is sadly all too possible that it could lead to some moral compromise which has far-reaching repercussions for family, friends, church and for the rest of life. Of course we can be forgiven, but it is another matter to rebuild trust and relationships and ministries. It is particularly easy in our sexualised culture to fall into sexual sin, which can be significantly damaging. It is not that it is more serious before God than other sin, but that the impact on others can be more long term and destructive because sexuality is so intimately bound up with who we are as human beings. Do everything possible to stay on the tightrope, but when you are losing your balance, *please* make sure you fall on the holiness side.

Balancing Acts

What does all this mean in practice for how we respond to culture – and to films in particular? Over the years, when I have run workshops on understanding films, there has often been someone who has protested that we do not need to make any response at all, saying, 'It's only a movie.' This implies that cinema is not a subject for serious consideration, and that our encounter with it should be simply at the level of entertainment. Others suggest that movies only have value if we can find some hook for the gospel within them. I do not accept either of these positions since they express conformist and escapist attitudes respectively. The third way is that of positive critical engagement. We can still enjoy films as entertainment, but I would argue that we should never approach them as *simply* entertainment. Our critical faculties must be fully operational even as we are enjoying ourselves.

The great biblical example is Paul's visit to Athens.[25] In the first half of Acts 17 we see Paul's normal pattern of visiting the synagogue in each city and using Scripture to show that Jesus is the Christ. When he reaches Athens, however, although Paul does visit the synagogue, Luke focuses on the time he spends in the public arena. First we read about him debating in the market place at the heart of Athens with advocates of the popular Epicurean and Stoic worldviews. Paul is summoned to the Areopagus – the council of Athens which took its name from its original location[26] – to explain the 'foreign gods' he has been arguing for (v. 18).[27]

Luke gives us just a brief summary of Paul's speech[28] which has three key features: he identifies points of contact and agreement (with both Stoics and Epicureans), establishing common ground; he identifies points of disagreement and tension (again, with both groups), challenging his audience's beliefs; and he argues for the truth of Christian claims. Lars Dahle says that, 'a crucial part of Paul's apologetic strategy seems to have been to affirm both Stoic pantheism and Epicurean deism as equally inadequate "half-truths", stressing divine immanence or divine transcendence at the expense of the other.'[29] Alister McGrath calls this a 'powerful apologetic device that enables Paul to base himself on acceptable Greek theistic assumptions while at the same time going beyond them.'[30]

Paul starts by noting that the Athenians were very religious (the word could also mean superstitious – a deliberate ambiguity) and refers to the altar dedicated to 'The Unknown God'. Notice that this is not something Paul has just seen in passing, but as a result of having, 'walked around and *looked carefully* at your objects of worship' (v. 23 my italics). It is the Athenians' admission of ignorance about divine things, and an indication that they are concerned to avoid incurring the wrath of some god which they have not allowed for in their pantheon. It gives Paul a point of contact which allows him to root his message in the context and worldview of his audience. He announces that he will resolve their ignorance – an offer which is guaranteed to make his audience sit up and take note. He goes on to discuss the nature of God and of humanity before finishing with a call to repentance – the means to avoid God's wrath.

During his message, Paul refers to Greek poets and philosophers. The most obvious references are the two quotations in verse 28. 'For in him we live and move and have our being' is attributed to Epimenides;[31] the second, 'We are his offspring,' is a quote from the Stoic writer Aratus.[32] There are also likely allusions to Plato, Euripides, Plutarch, Cleanthes and Aeschylus. And this is just in the brief distillation of Paul's speech which Luke gives us. Paul shows that he has given very careful consideration to the thinking and writing of both Epicureans and Stoics, and he genuinely engages with it. He knows the material well enough to take his thoroughly biblical message and express it in the thought forms, ideas and phrases that were part and parcel of his listeners' culture. Luke clearly intends Paul's engagement with his pagan audience in Athens to be a model for his readers – a model that has striking relevance in our secular culture in which many people have no biblical background.

Eyes Wide Open

Like Paul we must learn to be acute observers of the
culture around us, and the three aspects of his
communication need to become an integral part of ours.
First, we need to recognise that all truth is God's truth
whether or not it comes from the pen of someone who is
a Christian. We can affirm the truth that these rebellious
image-bearers have caught on to; we can celebrate some
of their insights; we can recognise when they ask the
right questions. There are points of connection and
elements of continuity; we can find common ground, not
least in our common humanity.

Second, we need to be clear and uncompromising
about the areas of tension and discontinuity so that we
can challenge those beliefs, values and attitudes which
are inconsistent with historical biblical Christianity. The
way we do this challenging is critical, though. All too
often Christians react aggressively – even violently –
against people whose ideas they disagree with. They
speak and act in ways that bring shame on the church.
Instead, we are to be like Jesus Christ who 'came from the
Father, full of grace and truth'.[33] Ranting and raving at the
godlessness or blasphemy of a film achieves nothing in
terms of changing how people think, and it almost
always closes off any future discussion. On the other
hand, Paul's approach of finding things to be positive
about first and *then* graciously but firmly challenging the
areas of disagreement can still lead to people rejecting
what we have to say, but it also earns enough respect to
open up potential for further dialogue.[34]

Third, as we highlight the positives and negatives, the
ultimate goal is for the truth claims of the Christian faith
to be clearly heard and understood. We must help people

to see their extraordinary relevance to the issues, hopes, fears and hurts of the world around us. The good news of Jesus Christ is always relevant, but the tragedy is that in a post-Christian western world many people (sometimes Christians themselves) do not realise how.

Film is an extremely potent art form, so movies are a great way of opening up this kind of dialogue. People love films and love talking about them, as we have noted already. Because they are for entertainment, movies are not threatening to people in the way that a church service might be. Most significantly, films touch on big questions. Every film examines issues of identity, morality, power, religion or sexuality, or explores the nature of happiness, freedom, love or spirituality. And thinking Christians should have plenty of good things to say on every one of them.

Notes

1 Truman's apparent walking on water and ascension into the sky are clearly parodying incidents from the Gospels. There are others in the film too, including 'burial', resurrection and perhaps a suggested echo of crucifixion.
2 There appear to be two continuity slips, however. In one very brief shot the number appears to be 138, and in a slightly longer shot it is completely absent.
3 Truman had previously pretended to be asleep in his basement.
4 Christof turned on the lights for daytime once it was discovered that Truman was missing.
5 Psalm 139:7–12.
6 It is worth noting that Christof's control room is behind the moon on the ceiling of the studio: he is the man in the moon. It seems to be suggesting an analogy between this

childhood figure of make-believe with the idea of God: something that we ought to grow out of.

7 Luke 10:27.

8 UNESCO (United Nations Educational, Scientific and Cultural Organization) Universal Declaration on Cultural Diversity, 21 February 2002 – www.unesco.org/education/imld_2002/unversal_decla.shtml.

9 See also Psalm 8:4–8.

10 Even to the extent that it was somehow bound up in the human rebellion against God (Rom. 8:19–22).

11 Cain's building of a city may be after the Fall and after his own murder of his brother, but that does not mean that the building of a city was a wrong thing to do. See Tim Keller, 'A Biblical Theology of the City', *Evangelicals Now*, July 2002 – www.e-n.org.uk/1869-A-biblical-theology-of-the-city.htm.

12 Nancy Pearcey, *Total Truth: Liberating Christianity from Its Cultural Captivity* (Wheaton, Ill.: Crossway, 2004) p. 47.

13 Compare Genesis 3:1 with 2:16–17.

14 It seems this is a result of having this doubt put into her mind – she is beginning to move towards the snake's position already. Or perhaps, feeling vulnerable to the temptation, she wants to establish the limits so strongly that she goes further than God had actually said.

15 D.A. Carson, 'Three Books on the Bible: A Critical Review', *Reformation 21*, May 2006 – www.reformation21.com/Past_Issues/May_2006/Shelf_Life/Shelf_Life/181/vobId_2926/pm__434/

16 Think of how strongly the Old Testament prophets condemn idolatry, often using the metaphors of adultery and prostitution to convey how offensive it is to God. See Jeremiah 2, Ezekiel 16 and Hosea 1–2, for example.

17 Ephesians 2:5.

18 James 3:9 (NLT).

19 Some Christians seem to think that if a Christian has made a film, it is above criticism. But how can it be? We may be redeemed but we are far from perfect and still struggle with our fallen human nature (see Rom. 7:14–25). Even the best

things we do are born out of a mixture of motives – it is so very hard to put aside our pride and self-seeking, even at the point of serving someone else in apparent humility. I would like to think that as I submit to God the writing of this book, for example, I would be writing solely for his glory and for the building up of his church. I would hope that everything about it reflects the image of God in me, an image renewed through my faith in Jesus Christ. But the reality is that I remain fallen and flawed. Even now, while I am seeking to serve God, my rebellion continues to reassert itself and my work remains tainted with self-promoting hubris.

20 For example, Brian Godawa, *Hollywood Worldviews: Watching Films with Wisdom and Discernment* (Downers Grove, Ill.: IVP, 2002) pp. 187–208; Peter Fraser and Vernon Edwin Neal, *ReViewing the Movies: A Christian Response to Contemporary Film* (Wheaton, Ill.: Crossway, 2000) pp. 65–71; William D. Romanowski, *Eyes Wide Open: Looking for God in Popular Culture* (Grand Rapids, Mich.: Brazos Press, 2001) pp. 121–135.

21 See Luke 7:36–50 and 15:1–2, for example.

22 Matthew 5:13–16.

23 2 Timothy 4:9.

24 Matthew 5:13.

25 Acts 17:16–34. After years of studying this passage, I am indebted to Lars Dahle for some new insights into it from his doctoral thesis, *Acts 17:16-34 – An Apologetic Model Then and Now?* (Doctoral thesis, Open University, 2001).

26 Areopagus means Mars Hill.

27 Bruce Winter explains: '. . . the Council of the Areopagus . . . sanctioned the official introduction of new gods to Athens. This involved the Areopagus engaging in an evaluation of the cult to see if these were genuine gods being promoted by the particular herald.' ('On Introducing Gods to Athens: An Alternative Reading of Acts 17:18–20', *Tyndale Bulletin*, Vol. 47 No. 1, 1996, p. 72.)

28 It takes about three minutes to read aloud, but we know

from ancient records that speeches to the Areopagus typically went on three or four hours, and Paul was not given to brevity (see Acts 20:9).

29 Lars Dahle, *Acts 17:16–34 – An Apologetic Model Then and Now?*

30 Alister McGrath, *Bridge-Building: Effective Christian Apologetics* (Leicester: IVP, 1992).

31 Epimenides, *Cretica*.

32 Aratus, *Phaenomena 5*. A similar line is found in Cleanthes' *Hymn to Zeus 4*.

33 John 1:14, see also v. 17.

34 Acts 17:32.

2. What Lies Beneath

Understanding the Message

An alien scientist is stranded on Earth where he is rescued and befriended by a young boy, himself rather a loner in need of a good friend. He takes him home, teaches him to communicate, and a touching relationship develops. But the alien is discovered and becomes the subject of a top-level investigation by Government agencies which discover a remarkable connection between the brains of the boy and the alien. The alien apparently dies, but returns to life and the boy helps him to escape the Government agencies and return home. *E.T. the Extra-Terrestrial* (Steven Spielberg, 1982) is a delightful, innocent story of friendship between two outsiders, and of the extraordinary bond which develops between them.

It is also a story that raises big questions over the nature of human beings. It implies that there is nothing remotely special about us: there are other creatures capable of self-consciousness and rationality; other beings which can be considered to be persons. That suggests that humans are not uniquely made in God's image, and perhaps therefore also implies that there is no God.

To understand the message of a film in a full and

meaningful way, we need to probe beneath the surface and give some thought to what it communicates at the level of *worldviews*. We saw in Chapter 1 that Paul was interacting with the two most popular worldviews of first century Athens, affirming truth and challenging untruth. It is crucial that we engage with films and culture at that level for the dialogue to have any substantial value or lasting significance.

Basic Instincts

A worldview is a person's set of most basic convictions – beliefs which affect everything else they think, say and do. It is absolutely central to who we are. Tom Wright says:

> Worldviews are like glasses. We interpret the world through them. They are like the foundations of a house: vital but invisible. They are that through which, not at which, a society or individual normally looks; they form the grid through which humans organise reality.[1]

Many people have never reflected on what their worldview is – or even on the fact that everybody has one. In the same way as the foundations of a building determine much about its structure yet remain out of sight under the ground, our worldviews determine much about our lives without ever being noticed, never mind examined. Only when there are problems – with the building or with life – do we start to dig down and look closely. However, if we want to engage meaningfully with films or other aspects of culture, it is vital that we learn to do so. James Sire writes:

On one issue I remain constant: I am convinced that
for any of us to be fully conscious intellectually we
should not only be able to detect the worldviews
of others but be aware of our own – why it is ours,
and why in light of so many options we think it is
true.[2]

The analogy of worldviews as glasses reveals how they
affect us.[3] Imagine being so used to wearing spectacles
that you forget they are there. Whether or not you are
aware of them, they radically affect the way you view the
world around you. Everybody's worldview – their lens
prescription, if you like – is particular to them. Our
worldviews are products of our society, upbringing and
education, of the books we have read and films we have
watched, the experiences we have had and much more
besides. Compare spectacles with someone who has a
similar prescription and you will not notice much
difference. But compare them with those of someone
whose eyes are very different and you might not be able
to focus on anything. It is the same with worldviews. If
you compare your worldview with someone who
broadly shares the same convictions as you, it will seem
comfortable and familiar. But if you compare your
worldview with someone from another religious
tradition you might wonder how that person can make
sense of the world. They probably feel the same way
about you.

Λ word to the Whys

Worldviews are the convictions upon which everything
else rests. When my oldest son Charlie was a little boy

going through the tiresome phase of asking 'Why?' about everything, I discovered by chance that he was content if I responded, 'It's because of the weather.' It didn't seem to matter what the subject under discussion was, if Daddy said that it was due to the weather then no further inquiry was necessary. I kept this going for some time until the day I demonstrated my strategy to my wife who found it hilariously funny. Charlie never fell for it again – which was probably as well, although slightly dis-appointing. For a while, though, it was his worldview. This was the bottom line; no more fundamental explana-tion was possible. To an adult, it seems an amusingly irrational view of the world, but three-year-olds are only just beginning to construct a framework for under-standing reality. Almost everything Charlie had so far experienced in his life would have appeared to be caused by another person: food, clothes, entertainment, even sleep were things over which his parents seemed to have control. But parents have no control over the weather. And if sun and rain make plants grow, then maybe the weather is the cause of everything which his parents are not responsible for.

Our most basic convictions about reality form in a number of ways: as a result of experience, from what we have heard and accepted from others, perhaps partly from logical deduction. But at the end of the day, the most foundational of these beliefs are taken on at least a measure of faith. They do not rest entirely on other beliefs (although we may have some corroborative evidence). If they did, *these* more fundamental beliefs would be our bottom line, our foundation. In other words, the basis of all our beliefs, thoughts, actions and values is something held onto by faith as much as rationality.

Spanish film-maker Luis Buñuel was a surrealist and

an atheist. He wanted to undermine what he perceived to be a cruel, hypocritical bourgeoisie and all the institutions and values connected with it – things most people took for granted, like the church. He said, 'The purpose of surrealism was not to create a new literary, artistic, or even philosophical movement, but to explode the social order, to transform life itself.'[4] The morality of surrealism was an 'aggressive morality based on the complete rejection of all existing values.'[5] Buñuel rejected faith in God and any spiritual dimension, but his life was based on faith nevertheless: he was passionately committed to his belief in the value of surrealism even as it denied the value of everything. He wrote: 'all our thoughts and actions seemed justifiable; there was simply no room for doubt. Everything made sense.'[6] Bizarrely irrational as it may appear to many, from the inside Buñuel's worldview was reasonable and all-embracing. The multi-talented actor, writer and director Peter Ustinov was a very different kind of atheist. He was a rationalist. He believed that, 'The habit of religion is oppressive, an easy way out of thought.'[7] But he was no less a man of faith. He believed in the capability of human minds to discover truth for themselves. But with nothing outside of the system (i.e. God) to guarantee that our minds are able to think freely and discover truth, we cannot be at all sure of the validity of human reason – it is a matter of faith.

For an atheist, there can be no more fundamental explanation of why the universe exists other than to say, 'It just does.'[8] For a Christian, the answer is because of God's creative activity (however one understands that). But if the atheist asks why God exists, a Christian can only respond, 'He just does.' Both atheists and theists can talk about evidence for their position, but evidence is not proof. At the end of the day, these views on the existence of matter/energy and of God are assumptions which form the bedrock of every other belief we have. We call them *presuppositions.*

Life Through a Lens

Worldviews are not just about ideas though, but about how we live. James Sire's classic book on worldviews, *The Universe Next Door,* was first published in 1976. In recent years he has developed a fuller, more rounded understanding of worldviews, particularly influenced by David Naugle who emphasises the 'striking similarity between the biblical concept of the heart and the worldview concept'.[9] Sire gives this helpful definition:

A worldview is a commitment, a fundamental orientation of the heart, that can be expressed as a story or in a set of presuppositions (assumptions which may be true, partially true or entirely false) which we hold (consciously or subconsciously, consistently or inconsistently) about the basic constitution of reality, and that provides the foundation on which we live and move and have our being.[10]

Philosopher John Kok says:

Our *talk* (confessed beliefs or cognitive claims) is one thing, and our *walk* (operative beliefs) is another and even more important thing. A lived worldview defines one's basic convictions; it defines what one is ready to live and die for.[11]

The relevance of this for our attempt to engage constructively with movies can hardly be over-estimated. Since worldviews are so much at the core of our being (the orientation of our hearts), they impact everything we do. Of particular relevance to this book is that all our creative acts are shaped by our worldview. Films, books, music or art are all expressions of their creators' worldview. One writer may set out to explicitly communicate a worldview and argue for it; another may work hard at being objective, but it is impossible to achieve this completely and the worldview still seeps through. So when we set out to engage with a film, it is vital that we engage with it at a worldview level.[12]

It is one thing to be aware of worldviews, but we need to be able to identify them, understand them and respond to them. There are four key aspects to this – a process called positive deconstruction.[13] We need to analyse the worldview and evaluate it. As we do so, we must celebrate the good and challenge the bad.

Analyse the Worldview[14]

First, we need to identify the worldview we are encountering in the film. That does not necessarily mean knowing the precise meaning of terms like existentialism. Indeed, there can be a danger in viewing everything only in terms of such broad worldview categories because one fails to allow for the deeply individual nature of worldviews. What we need to do is identify and analyse the view of reality with which we are presented: what beliefs, values and attitudes underpin what we are hearing. Where is the writer or director – or my friend – coming from? It *is* helpful to be familiar with the broad worldview categories, but more helpful to know what questions to ask of any worldview, any person or any film.

Various writers have suggested frameworks for considering worldviews. I use a set of five questions which I formulated some years ago, drawing on Sire's seven basic questions[15] and Brian Walsh and Richard Middleton's four questions.[16] More recently, David Burnett's perspective[17] has enriched my thinking on worldviews, as has Sire's significant re-evaluation of the concept in *Naming the Elephant.* Note that my five key questions are really headings – an easily-remembered framework which opens up many specific sub-questions. I keep this framework in mind every time I watch a film, read a book or have a significant conversation.

1. What is reality?

Is the physical world all there is, or is there a spiritual dimension as well? Which is more important? Or is the physical world an illusion? Why is the world like it is? Where did it come from? What kind of God or gods are there, if any? Is time linear or cyclical? Does time even mean anything?

The question about reality is the most foundational of my five questions.[18] While the others are integral parts of the worldview, they all, in some sense, follow on from this question of what really is real. It is a question about *ontology* – about *being;* about what reality *is* and what it is like. *The Exorcism of Emily Rose* (Scott Derrickson, 2005) is one of many films which explore this area. It centres around the trial of a priest (Tom Wilkinson) charged with causing the death of a young woman (Jennifer Carpenter) in an attempt to exorcise her demons. The trial hinges on whether or not it might be possible that demons really exist. In other words, it is about reality: is there a spiritual realm? Or is the material world all there is? In *Mission to Mars* (Brian De Palma, 2000) a group of astronauts view a reconstruction of the history of life on earth. They are surprised to discover that life originally came to our planet from elsewhere in the universe – refugees from a cataclysm engulfing an ancient and intelligent alien civilisation. The implication here is that you do not need God to explain life, just science.[19]

2. What does it mean to be human?

What are the distinctive things – if any – about human beings? What is the point of life? Where did we come from? What happens when we die? Are some human beings more important than others? What does community mean? How should we relate to each other?

This is another huge question and is also about ontology. And again, many films deal explicitly with this theme. *I, Robot* (Alex Proyas, 2004), for example, questions whether there is anything unique about humanity. Could an artificially-intelligent robot develop emotions and the ability to dream? That is, could it *become* a person, worthy of being considered as equal to a human in every way, except biologically? *The Island* (Michael Bay, 2005) asks a similar question about clones who are biologically human but who lack (in theory) some basic human traits. Films like *Flatliners* (Joel Schumacher, 1990), *What Dreams May Come* (Vincent Ward, 1998) and *The Sixth Sense* (M. Night Shyamalan, 1999) more specifically explore possibilities of life after death. An enormous variety of films explore the purpose of human life – *It's a Wonderful Life* (Frank Capra, 1946) and *American Beauty* (Sam Mendes, 1999), for example. Others examine communities – *Chocolat* (Lasse Hallström, 2000), *Crash* (Paul Haggis, 2004) and *Hotel Rwanda* (Terry George, 2004) are just three contrasting examples.

3. How do we know what the good is?

Is there such a thing as good and evil? How do we know what is right and wrong? Should we be concerned primarily with the consequences of our actions, with ethical principles, or being a good person? What values should we live by? What do goodness or beauty mean?

This question deals with issues of *ethics* (though I also include aesthetics here). There are three basic approaches to ethics: *consequentialist ethics* focuses only on the consequences of an action – the end justifies the means; *virtue ethics* puts the emphasis not on the outcome but on what kind of person one ought to be; *deontological ethics* is about principles and duty. Many films deal with ethical issues at some level or other – especially those which focus on the nature of human beings. *Vera Drake* (Mike Leigh, 2004), *Million Dollar Baby* (Clint Eastwood, 2004) and *The Sea Inside* (Alejandro Amenábar, 2004) powerfully examine consequentialist ethics, the former also stressing virtue ethics.[20] These films are notable for their refusal to give trite answers to acutely painful issues. The history of film contains many potent and inspiring examples of characters motivated by duty or by fundamental ethical principles. One of the greatest is the lawyer Atticus Finch (Gregory Peck) in *To Kill a Mockingbird* (Robert Mulligan, 1962). When a mob gathers to lynch the black man Finch has controversially agreed to defend, Finch faces them down because he believes that all men are equal and deserve a fair trial. Having presented overwhelming evidence of the man's innocence, he pleads with the all-white jury to do their duty and acquit him. They do not do so, but the rightness of Finch's perspective is powerfully communicated.

4. How do we know anything at all?

Why do we believe the things we do? What are good and bad reasons for believing? How do we know what is true? Can something only be true if we have scientific evidence for it, or are there other kinds of truth? Where does wisdom come from? Where does meaning come from?

This question deals with the philosophical issue of *epistemology* or knowledge. This is often the hardest of the five questions to think about, and it is one which film-makers seem less inclined to tackle explicitly. *Memento* (Christopher Nolan, 2000), *Signs* (M. Night Shyamalan, 2002), *I Huckabees* (David O. Russell, 2004) and *Minority Report* (Steven Spielberg, 2002) are four which do to a very large extent. But it is an issue which nevertheless crops up to some degree within many films. *The Thin Blue Line* (Errol Morris, 1988) is a documentary about an innocent man's wrongful conviction for murder. It explores how self-interest results in 'truth' being invented. Self-deception is a common idea in films. One example is *The Prime of Miss Jean Brodie* (Ronald Neame, 1969) in which a teacher (Maggie Smith) imagines that she is educating her students but is in fact brainwashing them, with terrible consequences. Courtroom dramas raise many issues in this area: the need for evidence, the reliability of witnesses, and the power of rhetoric in shaping ideas, for example. *Twelve Angry Men* (Sidney

Lumet, 1957) is particularly interesting as it focuses on the deliberations – and manipulation – of a jury in a homicide case. Initially, all but one man (Henry Fonda) are convinced of the defendant's guilt, but he argues passionately that there is reasonable doubt. The entire film, bar just three minutes, is set in the jury room.

5. *What is the fundamental problem confronting all human beings, and what is the solution?*

What is the basic problem which stops us being fulfilled? How can we overcome this to be fulfilled? What do we most need in life? What is the nature of evil? How can we be saved from it?

This question has elements of ontology, epistemology and ethics within it – or at least, the possible answers are within these areas. A Buddhist would argue that human problems are a result of our preoccupation with the physical world and that we need to become enlightened. This is partly ontological (the claim that the physical world is illusory), partly epistemological (the claim that trying to know and understand is part of the problem), and partly ethical (some ways of living are appropriate because they lead to enlightenment). This question focuses our attention on why a particular worldview demands our attention.

Within films, there is often an implicit, if not explicit, suggestion of a right way to live and think in order to be happy, fulfilled or complete, or a way to be redeemed in some sense from the problems which humans face. *Amélie* (Jean-Pierre Jeunet, 2001) has a clear message that the world can be made a better place by an accumulation of acts of kindness to other people. *Gandhi* (Richard Attenborough, 1982) powerfully argues for the importance of peaceful resistance and simplicity of lifestyle.

You will not be able to answer every one of these questions for every film you watch. Many films, for example, never touch on the question of how we know things or why we believe things. However, by thinking carefully about each of these five areas, you will often be able to identify what is being *assumed* as well as what is being shown more explicitly. The difficulty here can be spotting what is assumed generally within our culture – especially if it is an assumption we also share. Sociologist Peter Berger says that cultures have what he calls 'plausibility structures' – deep-rooted ways of thinking that make some ideas seem reasonable and others unthinkable. They become so integral to our thinking as we grow up that we find it difficult to notice, never mind question them. It is simply inconceivable for us to think in any other way. Western societies, for example, assume that human beings are individual and independent from each other: 'Once a baby is born any linkage between the mother and child is merely social. There is no mystical link with the family lineage as is common in traditional societies.'[21] If the characters in a film rely for their knowledge entirely on empirical evidence and logical reasoning – Douglas Quaid (Arnold Schwarzenegger in Paul Verhoeven's 1990 film *Total Recall*), for example – we may not notice it at first. The film may not explicitly deny God and the possibility of revelation, but it may well just assume that such things are not part of normal life.

Evaluate the Worldview[22]

Having identified the beliefs, values and attitudes that

are being communicated through a particular film, or those that shape the communication, we need to evaluate them. Which can we be positive about because they are consistent with a Christian worldview, and which do we need to be more critical of? So we have some more questions to ask.

Coherence

Do the ideas *cohere?* That is, do they hang together and make sense? Which ones do and which do not? Something which does not make sense cannot be true. *Mulholland Dr.* (David Lynch, 2001) appears at first to be a conventional linear narrative and we take it at face value. However, when a singer collapses mid-song – and the song continues, we get our first major clue that what we have seen is not the true story. From this point on, it becomes increasingly difficult – eventually impossible – to work out what is happening. It no longer makes sense and can therefore no longer be considered a true account (within the framework of the film, that is, not a true story from the real world). And indeed it is not. What we have witnessed is an increasingly tortured dream arising out of a dreadfully guilty conscience.[23]

So something which does not make sense cannot be true. And something which is true should make sense. However, we do need to allow for the possibility of a paradox as opposed to a contradiction. We are dealing with a contradiction if two statements cannot both be true (Woody Allen is a film director; Woody Allen is not and never has been a film director), but it is a paradox if there are good reasons for believing two statements to be true, but we cannot see the right way to reconcile them. A classic example is the fact that certain experiments in physics clearly demonstrate that light is a wave; other experiments clearly show that light is composed of particles. The two seem irreconcilable, but the evidence is so strong for both that physicists have to live with the paradox. A familiar theological example is the humanity and deity of Jesus. The biblical evidence is clear that he is fully human *and* that he is fully God. The problem is that our human brains are finite and are incapable of fully understanding the nature of God. Why should we assume that we ought to be able to understand it?

Pragmatism

Secondly, we need to ask if the ideas *work*. What happens if you push them a little further? What kinds of tensions and difficulties would you run into? Where does it all come crashing down? If a worldview is true we should expect it to work in practice – it should have some pragmatic results. It seems that for many in western society, this is the most important criterion for deciding whether something is true: if it works it must be all right.

However, it is a flawed approach. The world is a complex place full of complex people and what works for one person might not work for someone else. If all that matters is that it works for *me*, and therefore is true for *me*, the very idea of truth is robbed of its power. It results in relativism with everyone's version of 'truth' being equally valid.

Another problem is the difficulty of assessing whether something really does work. It is useful to believe all kinds of things (that I can do exactly as I please, for instance) but that does not make it true. Something might *seem* to work, but our belief about *why* it works could be fundamentally wrong. At the beginning of *The Matrix*

(Andy and Larry Wachowski, 1999), while Thomas Anderson (Keanu Reeves) was still connected to the Matrix, he believed that he was living in a normal world. It was a belief which worked, enabling him to live a normal life. He may have been dissatisfied with it, but he could not know that his understanding of the world was *untrue* until the rebels rescued him and showed him the reality of his situation.

Another difficulty is that we cannot know whether something will continue to work in the long term. Buddhism and Christianity both seem to work in terms of giving people a sense of peace, but we cannot know *from our experience* whether either of them continue to work after death. Until we are dead, of course.

So the fact that something works does not *prove* that the ideas are true, nevertheless, it is a useful *indicator* that they could be true and are worth closer consideration.

Correspondence

Thirdly, we need to ask, do these ideas *correspond* with reality? Do they describe the world as it really is? Or are they a distortion, or even complete invention? Do they ignore some significant factor? For many philosophers – especially Christian ones – this is the most important of the three criteria for evaluating worldviews.[24] The more truthful a worldview is, the better its description of reality and of human beings will fit with our experience. The more truthful its view of ethics, the more we are able to make good ethical decisions (which is why some people argue that asking 'does it work?' is really a subset of this question: if the ideas fit with reality, then you would expect them to work; if the description of reality is flawed, then you would expect practical problems to ensue).

The biblical understanding of humans as rebellious image-bearers explains what we see in human nature better than any other perspective – it explains why we can be so noble and good, and yet so selfish and wicked. Looking for correspondence with reality is not something confined to realist films. Fantasy and science fiction films and literature are sometimes profoundly true in their view of humanity and the problems we face, and their non-realistic context can help us to see the truth more clearly. *Beauty and the Beast* (Gary Trousdale and Kirk Wise, 1991) is an animated fairy tale for children, but who could doubt that it has much to say which is true on the subject of relationships and how we perceive others?

As we work through part two of the process, we need to be identifying where the ideas are correct and where they are incorrect. Like Paul in Athens,[25] we should be positive about points on which we agree and express clearly our disagreement on other issues. Tragically, it seems that all too often Christians are quick to condemn something but very slow to praise. As we evaluate the ideas within film in terms of coherence, pragmatism and correspondence, we are looking for truth which we can affirm as well as untruth which we must dispute. So parts three and four of the process do not happen consecutively after part two, but instead happen concurrently with it. I separate them out to ensure that we pay close enough attention to both aspects.

Celebrate the good[26]

If the ideas actually make sense, we need to acknowledge that fact, even if we profoundly disagree with them. A coherent worldview deserves to be treated with respect.

We need to engage with it critically but positively. We need to take seriously an approach to life that works, because others around us will take it seriously. And where a film or a worldview is a true reflection of reality, we need to acknowledge the fact. To do otherwise has two serious consequences. First, if other people perceive us to be continually disparaging, attacking or ridiculing ideas which seem to them to be true, they will soon hold Christians in contempt. Second, as Nick Pollard points out:

> Whether we like it or not, other worldviews contain truth. If we reject them totally, we shall find that, as well as rejecting error, we are also rejecting truth. And if we reject truth, we push ourselves into error.[27]

Paul tells us to 'Fix [our] thoughts on what is true and honourable and right. Think about things that are pure and lovely and admirable. Think about things that are excellent and worthy of praise.'[28] William Romanowski says that Christians

> . . . often employ this passage to defend whatever appears nice, heart-warming, and comforting over what is true, right and excellent. This has contributed to a preference within the church for popular art that is sentimental and melodramatic.[29]

He points out that the Bible includes accounts of 'the most heinous, violent, and immoral behaviour'[30] yet it surely meets Paul's criteria. He does not comment on the fact that in passages such as Ezekiel 16 and 23, God is not afraid to express himself in shockingly graphic terms. Romanowski continues:

The advice to the Philippians suggests an attitude and way of looking at things; in short, a perspective. . . . The virtues listed in Philippians are meant to serve as a guide for Christian discernment. This passage should be used not so much to limit artistic engagement but to open the whole world up to Christian treatment and evaluation.[31]

Thinking about what is true means recognising the grim reality of our fallen nature – 'the waste and ugliness of war and injustice, the depths of human despair, the chaos and confusion of life'[32] – as much as valuing integrity, compassion, and other Christian virtues. If a film has integrity in the way it highlights aspects of human fallenness (whether or not the film-maker understands things in this way), we should commend it. Thinking about 'things that are excellent and worthy of praise' means that we should applaud the emotional honesty of a film and its artistic excellence. In fact, Peter Fraser writes:

Our first concern should be *cinematic and dramatic excellence*. Regardless of the message of the individual film, Christians ought to be the first to recognize and praise a film's artistry. All beauty reflects God's beauty, whether it is understood to be from the Creator or not.[33]

In short, we are looking for anything which reflects the likeness of God: truth, insight into the nature of things and a right sensitivity to the difficulties, dilemmas and tensions of life. We are also looking for evidence of the longing for God which is innate in every human being. We were created to know him and worship him, and if we cannot do so we express that urge in many other ways. Our longings for happiness, love, freedom, fulfilment and peace are really expressions of our deeper longing for God.

Challenge the Bad

We must not, however, become so concerned to be positive that we neglect to point out those things which fall short of truth and excellence. There is strong pressure within western culture not to disagree with someone's beliefs or values – not to be judging someone. But to sweep disagreement under the carpet is not intellectually honest. It fails to treat the other view with respect because it refuses to engage with it in any meaningful way. Every worldview is reduced to a supposed lowest common denominator which fails to do justice to any of them. If I disagree with someone, the respectful response is neither to deride their worldview, not to diminish it. Rather it is to enter into dialogue so that I understand it more fully, attempting to see it from their point of view, so that we can both see exactly how and why we think differently.

It is important to remember that it is much easier to disagree with the worldview of a film than with a person. We all, consciously or otherwise, sit in judgement on every movie we see, and on the characters within it. Learning to challenge a lack of artistic excellence and integrity, or the values and ideas expressed within a film, can be something which opens up stimulating debate – especially when we are being positive about other things rather than expressing a knee-jerk response.

So we are also looking for error, for examples of human blindness and of people looking for the right things in the wrong direction. We are looking for those God-sub-stitutes which people chase when they cannot or will not pursue a relationship with the creator himself. We are looking for ways in which our rebellion against God is expressed consciously and unconsciously.

As I noted in the introduction, this process of engaging with worldviews in films (or with people) can seem daunting at first, and it does require some hard thinking. But it does get easier with practice, and after a while it can become second nature to engage with a film without this getting in the way of our enjoyment of it. I long to see Christians find this way of thinking becoming so much a part of them that they cannot help but watch films 'worldviewishly' – and so become far more effective at naturally sharing Christian perspectives on what they watch.

Notes

1 N.T. Wright, *The New Testament and the People of God* (London: SPCK, 1992) p. 125.
2 James W. Sire, *The Universe Next Door: A Basic Worldview Catalog*, fourth edition (Downers Grove, Ill.: IVP, 2004) p. 11.
3 The word *worldview* comes from the German word *weltanschauung* which means 'a view onto the world'.
4 Luis Buñuel, *My Last Sigh* (New York: Alfred A. Knopf, 1983) p. 107.
5 Buñuel, *My Last Sigh*, p. 107.
6 Buñuel, *My Last Sigh*, p. 107.
7 Quoted in Jonathon Green, *The Cassell Dictionary of Cynical Quotations* (London: Weidenfeld and Nicolson, 1994).
8 Stephen Hawking wrote: 'Although science may solve the problem of how the universe began, it cannot answer the

question: Why does the universe bother to exist? I don't know the answer to that.' (*Black Holes and Baby Universes* (London: Bantam Press, 1993) p. 99.)

9 James W. Sire, *Naming the Elephant: Worldview as a Concept* (Downers Grove, Ill.: IVP, 2004) p. 44.

10 Sire, *Naming the Elephant*, p. 122.

11 John H. Kok, 'Learning to Teach from Within a Christian Perspective', Pro Rege, June 2003, p. 12, quoted in Sire, *Naming the Elephant*, p. 38.

12 For more information about worldviews, see Burnett, David, *Clash of Worlds: What Christians Can Do in a World of Cultures in Conflict*, second edition (London: Monarch, 2002); James P. Eckman, *The Truth About Worldviews: A Biblical Understanding of Worldview Alternatives* (Wheaton, Ill.: Crossway, 2004); David Naugle, *Worldview: The History of a Concept* (Grand Rapids, Mich.: Eerdmans, 2002); James W. Sire, *Naming the Elephant: Worldview as a Concept* (Downers Grove, Ill.: IVP, 2004); James W. Sire, *The Universe Next Door: A Basic Worldview Catalog*, fourth edition (Downers Grove, Ill.: IVP, 2004).

13 Nick Pollard, *Evangelism Made Slightly Less Difficult* (Leicester: IVP, 1997) pp. 48–56. Note that the labels given to the four stages of the process in *Evangelism Made Slightly Less Difficult* are expressed differently in this book, but the methodology remains essentially the same.

14 Pollard expresses this as 'identifying the worldview' (*Evangelism Made Slightly Less Difficult*, p. 48). This seems to suggest finding the correct label to apply to a worldview as a whole. However, since many people feel that they do not have the knowledge to be able to do so accurately, and since such labelling has rather limited value, I think it is more helpful to see this stage as teasing out, or analysing, the component parts of the worldview.

15 Sire, *The Universe Next Door*, p. 20.

16 Brian J. Walsh and Richard J. Middleton, *The Transforming Vision: Shaping a Christian Worldview* (Downers Grove, Ill.: IVP, 1984) p. 35.

17 David Burnett, *Clash of Worlds: What Christians Can Do in a World of Cultures in Conflict*, second edition (London: Monarch, 2002) p. 35.

18 See Sire, *Naming the Elephant*, chapter 3.

19 It does, of course, beg the question of where the alien life came from in the first place.

20 For a discussion on the ethics of *Vera Drake* and *Million Dollar Baby*, see my chapter 'Killing Me Softly' in Tony Watkins (ed.), *Playing God: Talking About Ethics in Medicine and Technology* (Milton Keynes: Damaris, 2006) pp. 39–53.

21 Burnett, *Clash of Worlds*, p. 43.

22 Pollard expresses this as 'analysing the worldview' (*Evangelism Made Slightly Less Difficult*, p. 52). Analysis seems to suggest the kind of process described in the stage – identifying the component parts. This second stage is perhaps more helpfully understood as evaluation since we are trying to determine the truth or falsity of the ideas.

23 For more on *Mulholland Dr.*, see Caroline Puntis, 'Mulholland Dr.', *CultureWatch*, 2004 – www.damaris.org/content/content.php?type=5&id=347.

24 Others, like Hegel (1770–1831), argue that at the end of the day you form a *belief* that there is a correspondence between reality and your belief, and therefore you are no further forward.

25 See Chapter 1.

26 For parts three and four of the process of positive deconstruction, I have substituted 'celebrate the good' and 'challenge the bad' for Pollard's labels of 'affirm the truth' and 'discern the error' (pp. 55–56). While these are appropriate labels when talking about worldviews in terms of their belief content, they seem to be too narrow in the context of films. They focus our attention too narrowly on the intellectual dimensions of film, whereas we also need to be engaging with the emotional and aesthetic dimensions.

27 Pollard, *Evangelism Made Slightly Less Difficult*, p. 55.

28 Philippians 4:8 (NLT).

29 William D. Romanowski, *Eyes Wide Open: Looking for God in Popular Culture* (Grand Rapids, Mich.: Brazos Press, 2001) p. 142.

30 Romanowski, *Eyes Wide Open*, p. 143.

31 Romanowski, *Eyes Wide Open*, p. 143.

32 Romanowski, *Eyes Wide Open*, p. 143.

33 Peter Fraser and Vernon Edwin Neal, *ReViewing the Movies: A Christian Response to Contemporary Film* (Wheaton, Ill.: Crossway, 2000) p. 32 (their italics).

3. Modern Times

A History of Worldviews and Film

Film, like other media, has been influenced by every worldview around. Cinema was born in the late Victorian era but it was soon profoundly shaped by the modernism of the first decades of the twentieth century. In the fifties and sixties, existentialism inspired many film-makers and writers. In the postmodern culture of recent decades, film has once more reflected the dominant worldview of the time. In a chapter of this length we can only cross this historical landscape with a brief tracking shot. There are many worldviews which have impacted on film, but I am only considering the big picture of four major influences rather than zooming in on details.

The Christian Legacy

Film is a global medium now, but it was born and brought up in western culture, which has been decisively shaped by Christianity for centuries. The Christian faith was the biggest single influence on the western world until well into the twentieth century – despite the growing impact of the various intellectual movements which challenged it. It was ultimately the horror of two world wars which led to a widespread rejection of Christian faith, especially in Europe.

Nevertheless, the Christian worldview continued to shape people's thinking in important ways. Although people may reject the claims of Christ, the majority – even now to some extent – broadly share a Christian world-view. On the issue of reality, most British people still believe that it has both physical and spiritual dimensions, and acknowledge the existence of some kind of God.[1] They do not share the Christian view of humanity to the same extent, but ideas of human dignity, freedom and personal responsibility remain an invaluable legacy. In terms of how we know things, until relatively recently western culture shared the Christian understanding of truth as being absolute. The difference is that little credence was given to truth coming through revelation as well as through experience and reason. Morality, too, is still influenced by Christianity despite the moral decline in the west. We are acutely aware of ways in which society has become more permissive and promiscuous, but we sometimes forget that most people are generally decent, honest folk who think integrity and faithfulness are important. Few people are remotely aware of how much we owe to our Christian past in terms of how we think and behave.

The biggest departure from a Christian worldview concerns the fifth aspect of worldviews I discussed in Chapter 2: humanity's basic problem and its solution. There is little sense of our problem being rebellion against God – indeed, there sometimes seems to be minimal awareness that we even have a problem. Christianity is widely assumed to be just one of many possible ways of finding God. For many, the claim that Jesus Christ's death and resurrection can redeem us barely merits consideration. Nevertheless, a key aspect of the Christian heritage in the west is that these deeply-embedded beliefs and values still remain, though their influence grows steadily weaker.

There are other important aspects of the Christian heritage, of course. Most obvious are the various Christian traditions – especially those of Anglican and Roman Catholic churches. Related to this is the vast legacy of music, art, and architecture. Less obviously, the Christian influence on education, health care, science and politics is enormous. Each of these aspects has shaped most film-makers and their audience, at least to some extent. As we move on shortly to consider other worldview influences on cinema, we need to bear in mind this enduring legacy – even for those who are opposed to Christian faith.

In every generation, there have been film-makers who deliberately set out to express Christian truth and values. The earliest full-length film about Jesus may be *From the Manger to the Cross* (Sidney Olcott, 1912), but hundreds of films have since been made on other biblical subjects. Some of the most famous classics include *The Ten Commandments* (Cecil B. DeMille, 1956; he previously filmed this story in 1923), *The Greatest Story Ever Told* (George Stevens, 1965), *The Robe* (Henry Koster, 1953) and *Ben Hur* (William Wyler, 1959). Obvious recent examples include *The Prince of Egypt* (Brenda Chapman, Steve Hickner and Simon Wells, 1998) and Mel Gibson's *The Passion of the Christ* (2004). Not very well known, but immensely powerful, is Norman Stone's *Man Dancin'* (2003). Other films have dealt with broader questions of faith within a Christian framework. Carl Theodor

Dreyer's *Ordet* (1955) and *Diary of a Country Priest* (Robert Bresson, 1951) are two of the finest films ever made and explore this issue with great sensitivity. More recently, *The Mission* (Roland Joffé, 1986), *Breaking the Waves* (Lars von Trier, 1996) and *Bruce Almighty* (Tom Shadyac, 2003) have explored similar questions. Countless other movie-makers have consciously or unconsciously made connections with the Christian story or preserved Christian values. *Superman Returns* (Bryan Singer, 2006) is a recent example of a film which has done this very deliberately. Many Christian books and websites on film focus primarily on identifying these connections (see the Bibliography for details).

Naturally, there are always film-makers who seem to be rejecting Christian truth and values. According to some, *Monty Python's Life of Brian* (Terry Jones, 1979) and *V for Vendetta* (James McTeigue, 2005) should be understood in this way. Sadly, it seems that many Christians react aggressively against the slightest whiff of anti-Christian sentiment, slamming a movie as blasphemous and anti-Christian without pausing to consider what it is really saying. *Saved!* (Brian Dannelly, 2004) was condemned vociferously by a number of Christian groups[2] – but it is targeting mindless fundamentalism, not Christian faith itself. So, too, are *Life of Brian* and *V for Vendetta*. Most movie attacks on Christianity are not so much attacking faith itself as the ways in which human beings have twisted it. This is arguably even true of films like Martin Scorsese's *The Last Temptation of Christ* (1988) and *The Da Vinci Code* (Ron Howard, 2006) which appear to be more obviously challenging specific Christian beliefs. Much more common are movies promoting beliefs and values which are decidedly not Christian, though they do not explicitly attack Christian faith. It seems to me that the real problem with *Saved!* is the morality it advocates, not what it says about Christians. Scorsese was brought up a Catholic and constantly explores religious ideas in his films, but he seems to have turned his back on Christian beliefs and values. Speaking about his film *The Departed* (2006) he says:

Good and bad become very blurred. That is something I know I'm attracted to. It's a world where morality doesn't exist, good doesn't exist, so you can't even sin any more as there's nothing to sin against. There's no redemption of any kind.[3]

Yet still the Christian influence on Scorsese is significant – if only because he is reacting against it. Years earlier, the great Italian director Roberto Rossellini described himself as a 'religious atheist' because, 'he was willing to take on the ideas of Christianity in all their creative potency provided this did not include a belief in God'.[4] He is far from alone among film-makers in feeling this way.

So while Christianity does not have the place in western culture that it once did, its influence continues to be felt in many aspects of culture, including cinema. It remains a source of inspiration, imagery and ideas which film-makers repeatedly explore. However, over the last century or so, there have been some major worldview shifts within western culture. Perhaps the most significant of these is the rejection of the spiritual dimension which really began in the Enlightenment and is especially associated with modernism. For the first time in centuries, Christianity in the west had a serious rival for people's hearts and minds.

Modernism

Modernism, modernity and *modern* are confusing terms. Quite what they mean depends on who is using them, and in what context. *Modernism* primarily describes a particular movement in the arts.[5] *Modernity* is the period of history in which Modernism was dominant. In its most common usage, *modern* (literally meaning 'of today') refers to anything which is very contemporary, but it also refers to the period of modernity. That period was in many ways characterised by a particular worldview, however, which a number of writers therefore also refer to as modernism.[6] To try to reduce the ambiguity a little, I refer to the movement in the arts as Modernism (with a capital M) and to the worldview as modernism (with a minuscule m). My focus in this chapter is primarily on worldviews, but the arts movement is highly relevant, and it is helpful to understand a little of how both aspects of modernity came about.

The roots of modernity are in the Renaissance.[7] This is the time 'when we first encounter secular humanism, the notion that man (not God) is the measure of all things ... and "utopian" visions of a more perfect society.'[8] Such ideas really took off during the European Enlightenment of the seventeenth and eighteenth centuries.[9] The Enlightenment placed the highest value on human rationality, especially in science and logic. Reason, rather than revelation, became the primary means to know what was true and right. There was a growing sense that humanity was in charge of its own destiny, coinciding with the beginnings of the Industrial Revolution. It gave rise to a strong belief in progress, and a focus on innovation, freedom and happiness.

The Romantics Strike Back

This confident optimism continued on through the nineteenth century, though a note of scepticism crept in. Immanuel Kant (1724–1804) marks a significant change. He argued that everything we think we know about the world depends on ideas which are *already* in our mind. So although he still stressed rationality as the ultimate authority, he insisted that there are limits on the certainty of what we know. The Romantic Movement, which had begun as an artistic rebellion against Enlightenment rationalism, was further inspired by Kant's thinking. The Romantics believed that reason must not 'act as a gatekeeper that determines what aspects of human experience should be seen as valid pointers toward reality'.[10] Instead, they stressed emotion, intuition and imagination. Rather than welcoming industrial progress, they were nostalgic for a lost past.

Nevertheless, the focus on freedom, innovation and progress continued. By the end of the century, the feeling was growing that there had to be a break with the past – in particular, with its approaches to art. Artists like Edvard Munch and Paul Cezanne felt they could no longer go on repeating what had been done before. Art became less about the impressions made by the external world, and more about pure self-expression. The superiority of photography in representing reality made this shift inevitable. Early in the twentieth century, Wassily Kandinsky notably moved towards the abstract expressionism for which he is famous, and Pablo Picasso and Georges Braque developed Cubism. In music, Arnold Schoenberg shifted away from classic tonality and began to write atonal music. These figures were some of the first Modernists – the avant-garde who rejected realism and embraced disruption of accepted norms.

Film was a brand new medium born on the cusp of Modernism. It seems surprising, then, that the early Modernists seem to have largely ignored it. This is partly because film was a development from photography. Film is intensely representational: it is ideal for recording events, and this is how its first proponents saw its usefulness. The first film ever shown was the Lumière brothers' footage of workers leaving their factory. August and Louis Lumière, having patented their *cinématographe* in February 1895, shot this 46-second film on 19 March 1895. They first screened it publicly, with some other short films, in Paris on 28 December 1895. However, film did not obviously lend itself to abstraction, which was the primary concern of the Modernists. A second reason for the Modernists ignoring film is that it was 'still a fragile enterprise that depended very much on its popular audience'.[11] And that audience was largely resistant to the radical movements in the other arts.

The Two Strands of Modernism

There was a second strand to Modernism which affected architecture and design more than art. Rather than being anti-rationalist, it saw new technology as creating both the opportunity and the duty to create a better world. This strand of Modernism also turned its back on the past in favour of new approaches, technology and materials. Two of the key slogans were 'form follows function'[12] and 'ornament is a crime',[13] expressing a minimalist approach to design. These slogans – along with the commitment to exciting new materials and technologies – show that this side of Modernism was deeply rationalist.

Karl Marx, Charles Darwin, Sigmund Freud and

Friedrich Nietzsche had also begun revolutions in the fields of politics and economics, human origins, the human mind and philosophy of religion respectively. But it was the First World War which cataclysmically confirmed that the old status quo had failed. It dealt a grievous blow to the notion of progress as a continuous and unstoppable force. The anti-rational strand of Modernism became a major force in the arts. One of its key expressions, Dada, was a reaction against the war, the logic which led to it, and seemingly almost everything else. Dada embraced chance, irrationality and absurdity. It therefore also denied meaning and values. It was at this point that Modernist film-making took off.[14] From the German Expressionists came such notable films as *The Cabinet of Dr. Caligari* (Robert Wiene, 1920) and *Nosferatu the Vampire* (F.W. Murnau, 1922). In France, a group of film theorists (including Louis Delluc, Germaine Dulac and Jean Epstein, all influenced by Freud) started to make films themselves. Dulac's 1928 film *The Seashell and the Clergyman* was the first surrealist film. The most famous Surrealist film-maker was Luis Buñuel, who first worked as Epstein's assistant. His first film was *Un Chien Andalou* (1929), which he made in collaboration with Salvador Dali. It is ironic that these Modernists despised the inexorable progress of rationalism, yet they were optimistic about the progress of art thanks to their daring break with the past.

However, the rationalist side of Modernism grew in importance:

At the core of Modernism lay the idea that the world had to be fundamentally rethought. The carnage of the First World War led to widespread utopian fervour, a belief that the human condition could be healed by new approaches to art and design – more spiritual, more sensual, or more rational.[15]

This strand of Modernism dominated the design world.[16] It was very authoritarian, endorsing certain right ways of doing things. The rejection of the past, coupled with a commitment to progress, systems and authority, came to characterise the age. There was a strong sense that everything had to be made new. There was an emphasis on health, hygiene and efficiency. New techniques and materials, mechanisation and mass production were expected to transform the world. Films gave audiences a glimpse of the new world Modernism was creating, as well as the kinds of worlds it imagined.

> Modernist theatre and cinema was a laboratory for utopia, an arena for experimentation. Here designers could try out new materials, new ideas for mechanised or robotic bodies, and new ways of organising the body in space.[17]

One of the most significant German films ever made is Fritz Lang's *Metropolis* (1927). It had a huge influence on many science fiction films – *2001: A Space Odyssey* (Stanley Kubrick, 1968), *Blade Runner* (Ridley Scott, 1982) and *Dark City* (Alex Proyas, 1998) among them. It is thoroughly Modernist in that it presents a vision of a futurist technological city. On the other hand, it critiques the separation between the head (the masterminds of the new future) and the hands (the exploited workers who are forced to give their lives for the sake of building and operating it). The suggestion is that humanity's only hope is the heart which mediates between the two and allows everyone to work together for the good of all. It seems that Lang might have been feeling the tension between the two strands of Modernism.

It is clear that Modernism was more than merely an approach to art and design. It was an expression of the Enlightenment worldview – which is why, as I noted earlier, this worldview is sometimes referred to as modernism.[18] It rejected any spiritual reality, and emphasised human reason and individualism. It had utopian ideals and insisted on having the right foundations and methods in all branches of human endeavour. But its domination and arrogant rationalism was to be challenged by another global conflict.

Existentialism

After the Second World War came a period of rebuilding, prosperity and growing optimism. Modernism was reasserting itself. But the war had, once again, engendered a sense of despair and meaninglessness. Once more many people reacted strongly against rationalism and certainty. A highly significant way in which this expressed itself was existentialism.[19] Writers like Jean-Paul Sartre, Simone de Beauvoir and Albert Camus[20] in France, and Karl Jaspers in Germany, denied God's existence[21] and insisted that reason was unreliable. They argued that life had no inherent meaning: all we can say is that we exist, and beyond that we individually need to create our own purpose and meaning through the choices we make. Sartre famously expressed this as 'existence precedes essence'.[22] *What* we choose is immaterial, since values are entirely subjective – something is only valuable because someone *chooses* it to be valuable for them. All that matters, then, is that we accept our responsibility

to choose (we are 'condemned to be free'). We authen-
ticate ourselves through making a choice. Sartre wrote
that, 'Man is a self-creating being who is not initially
endowed with a character and goals, but must choose
them by acts of pure decision . . . [and make] existential
leaps into being.'[23]

Existentialism came to prominence through literature
and a 'café existentialism' sub-culture more than through
philosophy. It influenced a generation with its themes of
alienation, the absurd, choice, and authenticity. Samuel
Beckett, who lived in Paris at the same time as Sartre and
his circle, explored similar themes – especially absurdity
– though he did not think of himself as an existentialist.
In America, the Beat generation (notably Jack Kerouac,
William Burroughs and Alan Ginsberg) picked up on
existentialist themes. They melded them with their non-
conformist lifestyle and experimental approach to
writing, as well as their fascination with eastern
worldviews. The Beats' impact on American culture (and
therefore on all of western culture) has proved to be
enormous, influencing the counterculture of the 1960s
and every alternative subculture since then.[24]

Making Waves

Existentialism influenced cinema directly through a
radical film movement in France, starting in the late
fifties. The *nouvelle vague* (New Wave) was the product of
a group of young film critics: Jean-Luc Godard, François
Truffaut, Jacques Rivettes, Claude Chabrol and Eric
Rohmer. They all worked on the journal *Cahiers du
Cinéma* co-founded by the influential critic André Bazin.
Bazin was committed to Realism (use of long takes and

mise-en-scène rather than montage[25]) and influenced the young men enormously. They were also inspired by Alexandre Astruc's belief that the camera is an instrument for personal expression *(camera-stylo)*, and by Bertolt Brecht's Epic Theatre.[26] The worldview of these iconoclastic young film-makers came primarily from existentialism, and they introduced its pessimism and cynicism into the language of cinema. Their work had an enormous impact on film-making in Europe and in the USA. The *nouvelle vague* directors gave expression to the existentialist rebellion against forces within society which impose meaning on people. Since individual freedom is paramount within existentialism, the central characters of *nouvelle vague* films are 'often marginalized, young anti-heroes and loners, with no family ties, who behave spontaneously, often act immorally and are frequently seen as anti-authoritarian.'[27] Writing about the central characters, Michel (Jean-Paul Belmondo) and Patricia (Jean Seberg), in Godard's seminal 1960 film *À Bout de Souffle (Breathless)*, Aristides Gazetas explains:

> For [*New York Times* critic Bosley] Crowther, these two lovers were fearsome characters since their animalistic drives 'were completely devoid of moral tone, and they were mainly concerned with eroticism, and the restless drives of a cruel young punk.' But Crowther seems not to be aware that Michel was one of the first film antiheroes, the outsider from the fictions of Sartre and Camus, living immorally in an antisocial world.[28]

Michel is adrift in a world without God, free to determine his own meaning and morality. He steals cars for a living and feels no remorse when he accidentally kills a police officer. It makes him feel alive in the face of his awareness of mortality. Truth is optional but he still wants love and loyalty.

The impact of Godard's and Truffaut's films (especially Godard's *À Bout de Souffle* and Truffaut's *Les Quatre Cents Coups (The 400 Blows*, 1959) and *Jules et Jim (Jules and Jim*, 1962)) was enormous. They introduced new ideas, new approaches to film-making, and a new freedom. Britain also had a New Wave in the late fifties and early sixties. The key figures in this were Lindsay Anderson *(This Sporting Life*, 1963; *If . . .*, 1968), Karel Reisz *(Saturday Night and Sunday Morning*, 1960) and Tony Richardson *(The Entertainer*, 1960; *A Taste of Honey*, 1961). They shared with the French New Wave a concern for realism, and frequently expressed existentialist ideas in gritty working-class contexts. Other directors who were strongly influenced by existentialism include Robert Aldrich *(Whatever Happened to Baby Jane?*, 1962; *The Dirty Dozen*, 1967), Michelangelo Antonioni *(Blow Up*, 1966; *The Passenger*, 1975) and Ingmar Bergman *(The Seventh Seal*, 1957; *Wild Strawberries*, 1957; *Persona*, 1966). Hamish Ford writes:

> The relentless close-up of the face is a useful formal and thematic key to Bergman's work. In these frequent, almost embarrassingly close and radically elongated moments the viewer can see, think and feel existential sureties in different states of crisis – as we watch subjects reduced to pure flesh, bones, mouth, nose, hair and eyes.[29]

Most famously of all, Woody Allen has explored existentialist themes throughout his career, often parodying them at the same time *(Love and Death*, 1975; *Annie Hall*,

1977; *Hannah and Her Sisters*, 1986; *Crimes and Misdemeanors*, 1989; and many more). The sense of angst in the face of life's absurdity and the reality of death pervade his work.

Existentialism had been a powerful challenge to modernism, though in many respects it is a direct continuation of it. However, it gradually became clear that it had evolved into something that was sufficiently different from modernism to be given a new name.

Postmodernism

We have seen that Modernism arose from a desire to break with the past and find radical new ways of doing things. But the modernist worldview tended to insist on certain 'correct' methods. By the late 1960s it became apparent that in architecture and other fields, Modernism had become nothing more than a set of stylistic rules rather than a general approach or principle. In architecture, following the Modernist rules increasingly resulted in buildings which were dehumanising places. The Modernist principle of constantly modernising had been forgotten. Modernism came to be perceived as arrogant, controlling and stale. No longer was it avant-garde; rather it had become Establishment. A new Modernism was needed: *Post*-Modernism, defined in opposition to Modernism as something which comes after it and supersedes it. The term 'postmodern' was not new,[30] but in the late sixties and seventies it was used more widely – especially by Ihab Hassan and Leslie Fiedler in literature, and by Charles Jencks in architecture.[31] Postmodern style is a strong reaction to the sterility of the earlier movement's rigidly geometric design, conventional materials and functionality. It is marked by its plurality of styles and materials – by its playfulness. In many ways it exhibits the same anti-rationalist and iconoclastic focus as early Modernism.

Postmodernism, like Modernism before it, echoed wider shifts within culture at a worldview level. Soon it came to be seen as a worldview in its own right. These wider shifts are complex, however, and trying to pin down postmodernism as a worldview is notoriously difficult. Some people argue that it is simply an extreme version of modernism, and that we should properly only talk about *postmodernity* – the cultural conditions in which we now live. I have some sympathy for this view since postmodernism clearly grows out of some of the anti-rationalist aspects of modernism that I have mentioned. However, I believe there have been substantial worldview shifts (especially on the question of how we know anything) and postmodernism is justifiably considered to be a worldview in its own right, as we shall see shortly. What is clear is that the culture of postmodernity constitutes a backlash against the dominating, controlling nature of modernity. Likewise, the postmodernist worldview is a backlash against the perceived arrogance of modernism's optimistic belief in progress and rationalism. There are several interconnecting reasons for this backlash.

Past Imperfect

First, there was a widespread disillusionment with the culture of modernity. More and more people resented the strongly conservative social norms of the time (partly due to the influence of existentialism and the Beats). In particular, the American Civil Rights and Free Speech Movements gave voice to the deep sense of disenfranchisement felt by many. These conflicts echoed around the world, leading to student protests in Paris and Prague in 1968. On top of this, the Cuban missile crisis of 1962 and the USA's protracted (and increasingly excessive) intervention in Vietnam throughout the sixties[32] made people fearful of a major conflict between the superpowers. The modernist world had clearly failed. Related to this was a growing distrust of the products of modernity. Opposition to nuclear technology and a growing awareness of environmental problems were the most obvious signs of this. Technological advances contributed to a growing sense of alienation – from the natural world, from other people, from God (or from the spiritual dimension) and ultimately from ourselves. The myth of inexorable progress was in tatters.

Second, there was a growing dissatisfaction with modernist ways of thinking. This was fuelled by the rising influence of three men whom philosopher Paul Ricoeur calls the 'masters of suspicion':[33] Marx, Nietzsche and Freud. Ricoeur believed that the prevailing plausibility structures within society (modernist and Christian worldviews, essentially) were false. He argued that these three thinkers exposed the failure of modernism through their extreme doubt. Ricoeur used the phrase 'hermeneutics of suspicion' to describe interpreting everything in a suspicious way – especially claims made by those in positions of power who use such claims to maintain the status quo.

Ideas like those of Ricoeur – and other thinkers in philosophy and literary criticism – found their way into popular culture very quickly for three key reasons. One was that many more people were becoming students than ever before and were being exposed to the ideas of the masters of suspicion and the new thinkers. The second follows on: these students became the bright young talents entering the industries of mass communication, and so popular expressions of these ideas reached a large audience. The third reason is that the dissatisfaction with modernity and modernism made people very receptive to new ideas.

Suspecting the Usual

Some of these concerns are surprisingly similar to some of those expressed at the birth of modernism several decades previously. As well as the reaction against arrogant rationalism, there was a sense of needing to break with a conformist, stultifying past, and an openness to new ways of doing things. Everything was open to question or challenge – received wisdom, standard methods and sources of power. Nothing was fixed. This results in an extraordinary diversity of approaches to making films, as well as a cheerful plundering of material from contemporary culture as well as from earlier times. *Forrest Gump* (Robert Zemeckis, 1994) retells three decades of American history with Forrest (Tom Hanks) accidentally ending up as a pivotal figure. Quentin Tarantino's *Pulp Fiction* (1994) is a complex film which weaves several separate stories together. It refers constantly to myriad aspects of contemporary culture: other movies, burgers, Madonna, TV cartoons, and much more. A number of films reflect upon the production of media – especially movies. Robert Altman's bitingly satirical *The Player* (1992) is a prime example. It begins with a virtuoso eight-minute tracking shot around the studio which includes people talking about other famous tracking shots. Many stars – including John Cusack, Elliott Gould, Angelica Huston, Jack Lemmon and Julia Roberts – have brief cameos.

Postmodernism's questioning of the past has some extremely positive aspects to it. For one thing, it allows due attention to be paid to emotion and subjectivity. But it has also meant that western culture has become increasingly sceptical about everything. People are sceptical about authority and increasingly sceptical about truth. Along with the stress on individual choice and a new fondness for eastern ideas, this has made people resistant to the idea of absolutes in either truth or morality. Truth is seen as something which is created by society rather than discovered, and is therefore relative. It is personal and subjective rather than universal and objective. Little wonder, then, that many people have no time for big systems of thought or belief (so-called grand narratives or meta-narratives[34]). Many people think that modernism, Marxism and Christianity, for example, have all been tried and found wanting. So instead of people committing to one big thing, everybody has their own ideas and their own agendas. Jean-François Lyotard called this the 'splintering autonomy of micro-narratives'.[35]

This scepticism is clearly seen in *L.A. Confidential* (Curtis Hanson, 1997). It is set in Los Angeles in the 1950s – its context is a modernist world. But as the movie's tagline states, 'everything is suspect, everyone is for sale, and nothing is what it seems.' Hanson says that the film deals with one of his favourite themes, 'the difference between image and reality,' and that he was delighted to be able to deal with this theme in LA, 'the city of manufactured illusion'.[36] Ironically, the only prominent character who has a clear sense of who she is and what she is about is a prostitute (Kim Basinger) who is the double of a famous actress. Thomas Hibbs writes:

> The gap between appearance and reality pervades the story, tempting us to conclude that reality is nothing but perception, that the world has no substance but is rather a series of competing appearances.[37]

A number of films raise postmodern questions of identity – *Blade Runner* (Ridley Scott, 1982), *Mary Shelley's Frankenstein* (Kenneth Brannagh, 1994), *Fight Club* (David Fincher, 1999) and *Everything is Illuminated* (Liev Schreiber, 2005) for example. Others examine morality – including *Changing Lanes* (Roger Michell, 2002), *The Cider House Rules* (Lasse Hallström, 1999), *Phonebooth* (Joel Schumacher, 2002) and *Brokeback Mountain* (Ang Lee, 2005).

Many postmodern films raise questions about reality and truth. *A Cock and Bull Story* (Michael Winterbottom, 2005), *The Science of Sleep* (Michel Gondry, 2006) and *Kiss Kiss, Bang Bang* (Shane Black, 2005) are just three recent examples. Another, *The Blair Witch Project* (Daniel Myrick and Eduardo Sánchez, 1999), was an attempt to blur the boundaries between reality and fantasy through its low-key marketing which suggested that it was a true documentary. The questioning of reality also results in questioning the modernist assumption that there is no spiritual dimension. Spirituality is back on the agenda of western culture – one of postmodernism's greatest benefits – though frequently it is seen in pagan rather than Christian terms. It is explored in such varied movies as *Contact* (Robert Zemeckis, 1997), *A Life Less Ordinary*

(Danny Boyle, 1997), *The Fifth Element* (Luc Besson, 1997) and *The Exorcism of Emily Rose* (Scott Derrickson, 2005).

In the postmodern world, reality is thought to be something which we must interpret rather than something which has an authoritative explanation. One of the few wildlife films to have made it to the big screen in recent years is *Microcosmos* (Claude Nuridsany and Marie Pérennou, 1996). It is an elegiac evocation of the small-scale world of creatures like insects and snails. *Microcosmos* includes only two brief passages of narration. Both are very poetic and evocative rather than explanatory, and are spoken (in the English version) by the mellifluous Kristin Scott Thomas. The remainder of the film simply allows us to respond to what we see. It is in sharp contrast to most wildlife films in which a male voice of authority provides an explanatory voice-over.

If even the absence of narration in a wildlife film is bound up with questions of worldview, we can see why it is so important to be aware of the influences of beliefs and values. In this chapter, we have considered only four of the many worldviews which have shaped movies – and continue to do so. Even with these we have barely begun to scratch the surface. There is not enough space in a book of this size to deal with the impact of Marxism, psychoanalysis, neo-paganism, feminism and many other ideas on films and film criticism. Nor have we touched on the impact of non-western worldviews through world cinema. But we do now have at least a broad framework for understanding movies in relation to worldviews before we turn to considering how individual film-makers communicate their worldview messages.

Notes

1 In the 2001 census of England and Wales, 72% of the population indicated an adherence to Christianity, and a further 3% identified themselves as belonging to one of the other monotheist faiths (Islam and Judaism) which share Christianity's view on the nature of reality.

2 American critic Ted Baehr, for instance, commented that '*Saved!* is a bigoted, frontal attack on Christians, who are depicted as confused and mean-spirited.' (Quoted on www.religioustolerance.org/savmovie.htm.)

3 Martin Scorsese interviewed by Ed Pilkington, 'A History of Violence', *The Guardian*, 6 October 2006 – film.guardian.co.uk/interview/interviewpages/0,,1888375,00.html.

4 Tim Cawkwell, *The Filmgoer's Guide to God* (London: Darton, Longman and Todd, 2004) p. 4.

5 As I have intimated, the word can refer to other concepts which are outside the scope of this chapter. One of its first usages was to describe a theological movement which attempted to accommodate Christian belief to the rationalism of the late nineteenth century.

6 For example, Lawrence E. Cahoone, *From Modernism to Postmodernism: An Anthology* (Oxford and Cambridge, Mass.: Blackwell, 1996) p. 13.

7 Usually defined as the period from the fourteenth to the sixteenth centuries.

8 Christopher L.C.E. Witcombe, 'Art and Artists: The Roots of Modernism' – witcombe.sbc.edu/modernism/roots.html. Witcombe cites the publication of Sir Thomas More's *Utopia* in 1516 as a defining point in history.

9 Some people prefer to refer to the seventeenth century as the Age of Reason, and restrict the Enlightenment to the eighteenth century.

10 Steve Wilkens and Alan G. Padgett, *Christianity and Western Thought: A History of Philosophers, Ideas and Movements, Volume 2: Faith and Reason in the Nineteenth Century* (Downers Grove, Ill.: IVP, 2000) p. 24.

11 James Monaco, *How to Read a Film: Movies, Media, Multimedia*, third edition (New York and Oxford: Oxford University Press, 2000) p. 287.

12 This phrase is often attributed to the great American architect Louis Henri Sullivan (who actually said 'form ever follows function'), though it was first uttered by the American sculptor Horatio Greenough.

13 This was asserted by Austrian architect Adolf Loos in his 1908 essay 'Ornament and Crime' which had a major influence on the Bauhaus school. Bauhaus was an art and architecture school which operated from 1913 to 1933, first in Weimar, then Dessau and, for the last year of its existence, in Berlin. It was one of the biggest influences on Modernist design and architecture, partly because many of the people associated with it fled the Nazi regime when it closed the Bauhaus down.

14 At the same time, Russian film-makers including Lev Kuleshov, Sergei Eisenstein (*The Battleship Potemkin*, 1925) and Vsevolod Pudovkin developed an approach to film-making which became known as Soviet Cinema. The Soviet Union itself rejected Modernism, but Soviet Cinema shares many of the same concerns and emphases.

15 'Modernism: Designing a New World 1914 – 1939', Exhibition panel text, Victoria and Albert Museum, London, 2006.

16 Architecture was at the cutting edge of Modernism with designers like Le Corbusier, Ludwig Mies van der Rohe and Walter Gropius (two of the founders of Bauhaus), and Frank Lloyd Wright among others. Modernism dominated architecture from the 1920s to the eighties with its simplicity of style (the 'machine aesthetic') and use of mass-produced materials (concrete, steel and glass). Mass production brought Modernist design to the general public – for example, Marcel Breuer's famous Model B3 tubular chair (also known as the 'Wassily' chair as Breuer designed it for Wassily Kandinsky at the Bauhaus School in 1925) was the first chair made out of bent tubular steel. It has inspired countless imitators and is still available. A classic

example of Modernism becoming part of everyday life is the famous London Underground map designed by Henry C. (Harry) Beck which has been used (with additions) since 1933. Numerous common sans-serif typefaces date from this era: Eric Gill's 'Gill Sans' was the first of its kind to be widely distributed. Walter Benjamin's 1936 essay 'The Work of Art in the Age of Mechanical Reproduction' is a hugely influential analysis of the implications of mass production for values. See bid.berkeley.edu/bidclass/readings/benjamin.html.

17 'Modernism: Designing a New World 1914 – 1939'.

18 The Enlightenment worldview is usually referred to by philosophers as naturalism (since it maintains that there are only natural phenomena, not supernatural ones) or scientific materialism (to be distinguished from the lifestyle materialism which focuses on having wealth and possessions). However, to refer to it as modernism is legitimate. Historians are, in fact, increasingly referring to the period from the fifteenth through to the end of the eighteenth centuries as the early modern period.

19 Its roots go back to the philosophy of Søren Kierkegaard and Friedrich Nietzsche in the nineteenth century and Martin Heidegger in the twentieth. The literature of Fyodor Dostoevsky and Franz Kafka (and others) was also a major influence.

20 Camus denied being an existentialist, preferring to refer to his views as absurdism. However, he was part of Sartre's circle and held to essentially the same ideas.

21 Note that there is also Christian existentialism, inspired particularly by Kierkegaard, Paul Tillich and Martin Buber. Sartre put Karl Jaspers into this category too: though Jaspers denied the existence of a personal God, he was nevertheless influenced by mystical Christian traditions.

22 In a lecture given in 1946, Sartre said: 'What do we mean by saying that existence precedes essence? We mean that man first of all exists, encounters himself, surges up in the world – and defines himself afterwards. If man as the existentialist

sees him is not definable, it is because to begin with he is nothing. He will not be anything until later, and then he will be what he makes of himself. Thus, there is no human nature, because there is no God to have a conception of it. Man simply is. . . . Man is nothing else but that which he makes of himself. That is the first principle of existentialism.' ('Existentialism is a Humanism' – www.marxists.org/reference/archive/sartre/works/exist/sartre.htm.)

23 Jean-Paul Sartre, *L'Être et le Néaut* (Paris: Gallimard, 1943), translated by Hazel Barnes as *Being and Nothingness* (New York: Simon & Schuster, 1956), quoted in Aristides Gazetas, *An Introduction to World Cinema* (Jefferson, NC.: McFarland, 2000) p. 194.

24 Writing in 1955, celebrated American film critic Pauline Kael described American life as characterised by, 'a prosperous, empty, uninspiring uniformity'. She continues, 'What promises does maturity hold for a teenager: a dull job, a dull life, television, freezers, babies and baby sitters, a guaranteed annual wage, taxes, social security, hospitalization insurance, and death. . . . It may be because this culture offers nothing that stirs youthful enthusiasm that it has spewed up a negative reaction: for the first time in American history we have a widespread nihilistic movement, so nihilistic it doesn't even have a program, and, ironically, its only leader is a movie star: Marlon Brando.' (Pauline Kael, *I Lost it at the Movies: Film Writings 1954–1965* (New York: Marion Boyars, 1994) p. 45.)

25 *Mise-en-scène* is the placing of elements into the scene; montage is the assembling of successive shots. Realist approaches to film-making consider *mise-en-scène* to be inherently more truthful because meaning is derived from the interrelationship of things which are in front of the camera at the same time, rather than from the juxtaposition of things which may have no natural relationship. I consider these two approaches further in the next chapter.

26 Also known as Theatre of Alienation. Brecht argued that

the purpose of theatre was to present ideas rather than merely entertain. The audience, therefore, should be made to reflect critically on what they are seeing, and so actors should remain at an emotional distance from their characters (*Verfremdung*, or distanciation, sometimes referred to as the V-effect), constantly reminding the audience that they are watching a play, not reality.

27 Stephen Nottingham, 'The French New Wave' – ourworld.compuserve.com/homepages/Stephen_Nottingham/cintxt2.htm.

28 Gazetas, *An Introduction to World Cinema*, p. 201.

29 Hamish Ford, 'Ingmar Bergman', *Senses of Cinema*, November 2002 – www.sensesofcinema.com/contents/directors/02/bergman.html.

30 Literary theorist Ihab Hassan cites a number of uses of the term, even as far back as the 1870s (when John Watkins Chapman used it to describe what we would now refer to as Post-Impressionism).

31 Especially from the publication of his *The Language of Post-Modern Architecture* (New York: Rizzoli, 1977).

32 Officially, America's involvement began in 1955 with the sending of military advisors to train the South Vietnamese. It ended with the unilateral withdrawal of US troops in 1973.

33 Paul Ricoeur, *Freud and Philosophy: An Essay on Interpretation* (New Haven: Yale University Press, 1970) p. 32.

34 Jean-François Lyotard famously wrote, 'I define post-modern as incredulity toward meta-narratives.' (*The Postmodern Condition: A Report on Knowledge*, translated by Geoff Bennington and Brian Massumi (Minneapolis: University of Minnesota Press, 1984) p. xxiv; first published in French in 1979.)

35 Lyotard, *The Postmodern Condition*.

36 Curtis Hanson, 'Off the Record', featurette on the DVD of *L.A. Confidential* (Warner Home Video, 1997).

37 Thomas S. Hibbs, *Shows About Nothing: Nihilism in Popular Culture from The Exorcist to Seinfeld* (Dallas: Spence, 1999) p. 85.

Second Reel:
How Films Communicate

4. Making Movies

Film-makers and their Art

Anyone who has waited in a still-dark cinema while the credits roll and everyone else jostles out of the door, knows what an army of people is needed to make a film happen. However, few films involve quite as many as *The Chronicles of Narnia: The Lion, the Witch and the Wardrobe* (2005). One director, Andrew Adamson, brought to life the writing of five people (four screenwriters, including Adamson himself, plus C.S. Lewis whose novel they adapted). But he had a team of seventeen assistant directors and second unit directors. There were three executive producers (again including Adamson), two producers and a co-producer. There were sixty actors and thirty-three stunt performers. Six people wrote original music for the film. On the technical side, there was one cinematographer and two editors, four casting directors, one production designer, four art directors, one set decorator and one costume designer. Sixty-three people worked on make-up; there were forty-two people in the art department and thirty-nine in the sound department. The special and visual effects teams numbered a staggering 568 (including modellers, animators, creature developers, lighting specialists and more). 168 people are listed as miscellaneous crew (including more animators, orchestrators, a solo violinist, a jeweller, secretaries, accountants, grips, photo doubles, and other roles). These were managed by seven production managers and supervisors. That is well over a thousand people to make one film – without counting extras or orchestra members. Most films involve far fewer, but virtually all of them involve at least dozens of people.

It raises the question: who is telling the story – and whose story is it? Cinematographer, production designers, editors and sound editors all help in a variety of ways to focus our attention on certain elements of the film in order to communicate the message most effectively and powerfully. But they do not shape the story at a worldview level in the same way as do the screenwriter and director, and to a lesser extent the producer, editor and actors. Writers and directors are setting out to communicate *something*, and whether or not they want to explicitly convey a worldview through a film, their worldviews still shape both the story they tell and the way that they tell it. So in this chapter we move from focusing on worldviews to considering how some key contributors to a film communicate through it. I am not, therefore, going to explain what the other roles involve, what the difference is between a gaffer and a grip, and whether women can get jobs as best boys.[1]

The Producers

In many ways, the most critical people in a film's development are not the director or the writer, but the producers. They are in charge of the entire production process: success or failure is, to a very large degree, in their hands. Their role is to keep everything moving on until the final goal of a successful film has been reached. Producers are ultimately responsible for raising the finances and budgeting, for the crew and the actors – in fact, every aspect of the movie.

Sometimes a single producer oversees every aspect, but more often the various responsibilities are shared between a small number of producers. The big studios appoint producers who are accountable to executive producers (often studio heads) for their day-to-day decision making. With independent films, the producers have more freedom but carry more risk and responsibility.

The process usually starts with someone coming to a producer with an idea for a film or perhaps a complete script. Or the producer may come across a book which can be adapted for the screen. The producer hires one or more *screenwriters* to develop this material into a *screenplay*, and will first work with them to develop a *treatment* of the story. Once approved by the people who ultimately control the purse strings – the studio head or a financial backer – the treatment forms the basis of the screenwriters' work. A script will go through many drafts before the producers and director are happy to proceed with it as a shooting script, frequently with other screenwriters or script consultants brought in along the way.

While this is going on, the producer is also busy recruiting others to the project, starting with the director. This is the appointment which, more than any other, makes or breaks the film. The producer wants a director who has a good track record of making the right kinds of films, or who shows the right kind of creativity. It may be that a particular script requires a director who is skilled at producing explosive action sequences, or someone who is able to help actors turn in wonderful, psychologically deep performances. It is also important that the director is someone with whom the producer can work well since they will liaise on very many decisions from here on: locations, crew, technical issues and much more. This phase, before the filming starts, is pre-production, and it can be a long, drawn-out affair – sometimes taking years – which requires both patience and perseverance on the part of the producer.

Producers are often in a difficult position: on the one hand they are facilitating the entire process, and should be encouraging and enabling the director and screen-writer. On the other hand, because the producer is also responsible for the budget, there may be a need to rein in some of the wilder creative urges of director or writer. Peter Jackson's status in Hollywood as both producer and director is such that he can expect to command a big budget. For *King Kong* (2005) the budget was reportedly $207 million, though he made the three *Lord of the Rings* films for less than $95 million each. When Paul Haggis directed *Crash* (2004), the budget of $6.5 million was so tight that he used his own house and car in some scenes.[2] The budget is often the deciding factor when it comes to casting, with some stars demanding astronomical salaries, and others prepared to work for a very modest fee if the project is exciting enough for them.

Once rehearsals and shooting start, producers generally do not interfere much with the filming itself, but they do keep a close eye on progress, schedules, spending, crew, and so on. After the filming is over and the movie goes into post-production, the producer is again very involved, overseeing the editing and sound editing. A completed film is often given test screenings, and the reaction to these is crucial to the producer who may ask for further editing or even for re-shooting of some scenes. Finally, the producer is also involved in the distribution and marketing of the finished product.

The Man with the Golden Pen: Screenwriters

Occasionally, writers of original stories or screenplays are fortunate enough to be allowed to develop the script themselves. Those few screenwriters who also direct their own material are in an even better position. When Robert Duvall made *The Apostle* (1997) or Jim Jarmusch made *Broken Flowers* (2005), they wrote the screenplay and directed the films, and told the stories they wanted to tell. If they failed to communicate what they wanted to, the fault was theirs alone – assuming, that is, the producers gave them the freedom to do so. Barbra Streisand went the whole hog (if that is not an inappropriate metaphor) with *Yentl* (1983) which she produced, directed, wrote and starred in. Few screenwriters have such freedom, but if they are lucky the director may be in complete sympathy with what they want to communicate. Peter Weir was so committed to Andrew Niccol's vision in his screenplay for *The Truman Show* (1998) that the two of them spent nearly a year developing it together to get it just right.

As we have seen, screenwriters are frequently developing someone else's story. When Peter Jackson and his wife Fran Walsh set about the task of bringing *The Lord of the Rings* to the screen, there was already a story to work with – too much of it, in fact, even for three long films. The task facing Jackson, Walsh and the other screenwriters[3] was to reconstruct the story as a script, decide what to leave out, find ways of filling in the back story in a concise way, and write new material where necessary to make things clearer.

Final screenplays are not always as faithful to the original as *The Lord of the Rings*[4] for many different reasons. It sometimes happens that the screenwriter does not share the same artistic vision or worldview as the original writer of the story. The more people are involved in shaping it, the less likely that the story's message will remain intact. Producers may also ask screenwriters to change the story in very specific ways. When Chris Weitz wrote the screenplay for the first part of Philip Pullman's *His Dark Materials* trilogy[5], he apparently muted the religious aspect of the story in order to keep production company New Line happy. Weitz says:

> New Line . . . have expressed worry about the possibility of [*His Dark Materials'*] perceived anti-religiosity making it an unviable project financially. My job is to get the film made in such a way that the spirit of the piece is carried through to the screen, and to do that I must contend not only with the difficulties of the material but with the fears of the studio. Needless to say, all my best efforts will be directed towards keeping *HDM* as liberating and iconoclastic an experience as I can.[6]

Among the many aspects of the film industry which Robert Altman satirises in *The Player* (1992) is the commercial pressure on film-makers to have a happy ending. It shows writers pitching the idea for a film called *Habeas Corpus* to a producer, insisting that there should be no stars and no happy ending because, 'that's the reality – the innocent die.' But when we later see the ending of the finished *Habeas Corpus,* we witness Bruce Willis breaking into a gas chamber to rescue Julia Roberts from wrongful execution.

Having a story adapted by others can be a difficult experience for the original writer. When Roger Michell filmed Ian McEwan's *Enduring Love* (2004, scripted by Joe Penhall), he wanted to make a number of changes to the story:

> We showed [McEwan] drafts as they developed at script stage, and he made his views very clear – some things he liked, some things he didn't like. We changed what we thought we could change. He was extremely benign, if not always without criticism of what we were trying to do. . . . It wasn't until he came to see an early cut of the film that I feel that he really got what we were trying to do. I have a lot of sympathy for him, because it must have felt that we were taking his child and cutting it into pieces and putting it in a different order.[7]

Calling the Shots: Directors

The producer may be in overall control, but it is the director's name which is usually most closely associated with the film. Although in the early days of cinema, directors had complete creative freedom, by the heyday of the Hollywood studio system they had almost none, with the producers controlling absolutely everything. Particularly influential producers include David O. Selznick[8] and Irving Thalberg[9] who used to tell his film-makers: 'I consider the director is on the set to communicate what I expect of my actors. . . . You gentlemen have individualistic styles and I respect them. It's one of the principal reasons we want you here. But if you can't conform to my system, it would be wiser not to start your film at all.'[10] There were a handful of very distinctive directors, however – men like Alfred Hitchcock, John Ford and Howard Hawks – who had a completely free hand.

François Truffaut and his colleagues at *Cahiers du Cinéma* were immensely impressed with Hitchcock, Hawks and others (in contrast to French films of the time which they derided as *cinéma du papa* – Daddy's cinema). In 1954, he wrote an influential essay in which he argued that the *auteur* (author) of the film – almost always the director – mattered far more than the individual film saying, 'There are no good and bad movies, only good and bad directors.'[11] This has since been rejected by most critics,[12] but nevertheless it led to the process of re-evaluating the work of particular directors and recognising their distinctive 'voice'. There is still some value in the idea of an auteur, and the term is still used of directors like Cronenberg,[13] Woody Allen[14] or Joel and Ethan Coen[15] whose approaches are distinctive and who tend to deal with particular themes. While we may not be able to know with any certainty what a particular film-maker is trying to communicate, when a director (or screenwriter) keeps revisiting certain themes, it is certainly worth exploring the connections. Partly as a result of Truffaut's thinking, directors came to have a considerable amount of freedom again. But some directors – particularly those who are also actors, it seems – like to retain as much control and freedom as possible by being producers of their own films. Robert Redford, Clint Eastwood and George Clooney are three obvious examples.

The director is the one who shapes the creative vision of the film, often in discussion with the producer. Sidney Lumet says that the most important decision a director has to make is:

What is this movie about? I'm not talking about the plot . . . But what is it about emotionally? What is the theme of the movie, the spine, the arc? What does the movie mean to me? . . . What the movie is about will determine how it is cast, how it will look, how it will be edited, how it will be musically scored, how it will be mixed, how the titles will look, and, with a good studio, how it will be released. What it's about will determine how it is to be made.[16]

It is the director who has the final word on set during the filming, and who finally decides how each scene is to be set up, lit, filmed and played. Of course, he or she makes these decisions in close collaboration with the various artistic and technical specialists on the team and with the actors, making the most of the particular creative expertise which they each bring. Directors often have certain 'heads of departments' (especially cinematographer, gaffer, key grip, production designer and costume designer) with whom they work regularly and whom they trust to understand what is required and work out the best way to achieve it. During shooting, a director will particularly be in continual discussion with the cinematographer about the best way of filming a particular shot: what lens to use, what angle to shoot from, whether the camera should be moving or stationary, how the visual elements in the frame are arranged, and so on. Roger Michell says that, 'film is very,

very collaborative. It's almost as collaborative as theatre, and to say that the film belongs to the director is wrong.'[17]

Some directors, like David Cronenberg and Lars von Trier, come to the filming of a scene with no fixed idea of how it will work. Cronenberg has a set and a script, but rather than orchestrating a preconceived, detailed plan for the scene, he walks through it with his actors, cinematographer (usually Peter Suschitzky) and other members of the crew. This is the point at which Cronenberg decides how it all should look. Although he is in the driving seat, the process is very collaborative and Cronenberg is open to suggestions from any of the actors or crew, the key members of which he has worked with on many occasions. Ed Harris worked with Cronenberg on *A History of Violence* (2005) and says:

> The reason I wanted to work with David is because he's a filmmaker, he knows what he's doing, he has his own vision, and it's just fun to work with people that care about what they're doing. You just know somebody is in command there. Not that you can't come up with stuff, not that he doesn't listen to new ideas, not that he isn't a collaborator, but ultimately, it's his film. Everybody understands that and I like working that way.[18]

Other directors, like Alfred Hitchcock or the great Polish director Krzysztof Kieslowski, have an extremely detailed, meticulous approach to directing. Julie Delpy, who played Dominique in *Three Colours: White* (1994), recalls how particular Kieslowski was with the placing of a lock of hair:

> Of all the directors I've ever worked with, he's the only one who's been attached to such specific

details. I've never worked with anyone who's so attached to detail, who conveys everything in his film. It's all those details that give his film its soul. That links with what he said to me about the way he studies people. That's what he does in his films. All human beings have a language in their actions, details that nobody else has. That's how he manages to describe characters that are so specific and so human. It's his focus on detail. It's as though he's looking at things under a microscope. He studies people under a microscope. And it's that that makes him absolutely unique as a director.[19]

Mise-en-scène

One of a director's two main preoccupations while on set is the arrangement of the shots (the second, the performance of the actors, I return to shortly). Film is first and foremost a visual medium. Take away the sound-track and it remains film; take away the moving image and the soundtrack is something else – a different kind of experience. So films rely on compositional principles which are shared with all other visual arts. Each shot must be framed so that it works visually. Everything that contributes to this is part of *mise-en-scène* – a term from the world of French theatre which means staging (literally, 'setting in scene').

As with still photography, a cinematographer needs to be aware of the balance and interactions of various elements including light and shadow, colours, textures and space. There are choices to be made about camera angles and positions, what lenses to use and what should be in focus. Unlike still photography, though, the scene changes: things happen and characters move, so the cinematographer and director need to be aware of how the balance and interactions change during the shot. They also need to decide what format to shoot in. The traditional Hollywood format used a ratio of 4:3 (or 1.33:1, known as the Academy aperture and still the most common for televisions and computer monitors) and was ideal for close-framed, quite intimate photography. The classic Hollywood two-shot (two characters in the shot) worked wonderfully well in this ratio, so interior dialogue shots were the norm until the advent of widescreen in the 1950s. The extra width lent itself to landscapes and hence more location shooting, but it made two-shots much harder because the characters tend to be either some way apart or not making full use of the available space in the frame. It means that directors might be much more inclined to use framing devices such as doorways when they need to focus in on a single subject. It is a technique used to potent effect by Brad Anderson in *The Machinist* (2004) to convey a sense of claustrophobic isolation for the protagonist Trevor Reznik (Christian Bale).

Mise-en-scène is more than photographic framing, however. It includes the sets, costumes and lighting. A director has enormous control over what actually ends up in each frame of the movie. When filming on a constructed set, there is absolutely nothing in the scene which is out of the director's control. The set and costumes are created, by the production designer and costume designer respectively, to a brief given by the director. Sometimes a director will provide only the broadest framework and then give the designers complete freedom. When Kirk Jones was directing *Nanny McPhee* (2005), he trusted production designer Michael Howells and costume designer Nic Ede to create something completely unconventional and riotously vivid, but entirely appropriate for the film. The house and small village in this charming film may appear to be a completely authentic example of timeless rural England, but every bit of it was built from scratch. Jones may have given his designers great freedom, but you can be sure that he still had to approve the plans before anything was constructed. On the other hand, a director may be very specific about the required look from the outset, as with Tim Burton who sketched out himself how he wanted the puppet figures to look in *The Corpse Bride* (2005). Some directors, like Peter Weir, have a reputation for being concerned with every last detail.

Shooting on location obviously imposes limits on what can be modified, but the locations are chosen carefully in the first place, and even the real world can be transformed beyond recognition. For a period film, it is easy to cover the road in gravel and horse droppings, but the houses may need repainting in authentic colours and things like street signs, lamp posts, telephone wires and television aerials may need to be removed or disguised. If such physical transformations are not possible, special effects can be used to change the background. Some or all of the background can be removed and replaced with film of another scene entirely. These days it is mostly done digitally, with actors often working in front of green (or other coloured) screens which are later replaced by background imagery (real or computer generated).

The decisions about what will appear in each scene may be taken by the production designer, but they are often at the instigation of, or in close collaboration with, the director. It is often worth asking why they make these decisions since they are very deliberate. Things may be placed into scenes as motifs – the recurring death's head moth in *The Silence of the Lambs* (Jonathan Demme, 1991), echoed by the butterfly wallpaper in the bedroom of Hannibal Lecter's (Anthony Hopkins) first victim, for example – or as a foreshadowing of something to come. The tracking shot right through the mirror early on in *Secret Window* (David Koepp, 2004) hints at the trick in perception that will come at the end of the film. Similarly, the zoom in to the pillow at the beginning of *Mulholland Dr.* (David Lynch, 2001) might alert us to the fact that we are about to witness a dream – though we may well not notice its significance at the time.

Casting Around: Actors

Once filming has started, the director's principal task is to draw out the best performances from the actors, enabling them to bring the story to life. The actors are the storytellers we see, hear and respond to. They are not the director's puppets, but bring themselves, their personalities and insights and skills to bear on communicating the film's message. While some directors, like Kieslowski, are very controlling of their actors, others, like Ken Loach, allow them to shape the performance in significant ways, often encouraging improvisation while filming. Mike Leigh works with the cast over a period of weeks as they improvise material within a basic story framework. This way they develop the characters and some of the storyline before filming. Both Loach and Leigh like to reveal the story progressively, so that the actors are able to respond to plot developments in the way that the characters would have done. Leigh does this in his pre-shooting workshops; Loach, very unusually, films the story in sequence rather than in a jumbled order determined by location or an actor's availability.

Regardless of the directing style, the best actors do not simply mimic life in their portrayal of a character, they incarnate the role in some sense and bring it to life. Many of the finest actors are known for immersing themselves totally in the role so that they effectively become the character. This tends to be known as *method acting*[20] and emphasises psychological and emotional realism through understanding the motives as well as the state of mind of the character. One approach encourages actors to recall similar emotional experiences of their own; another stresses such a deep understanding of the character's goals that the appropriate emotional response comes instinctively. A notable example is Robert de Niro. For his Oscar-winning role as former boxer Jake La Motta in *Raging Bull* (Martin Scorsese, 1980), De Niro not only gained sixty pounds in weight, but also underwent extensive boxing training along with co-star Joe Pesci – including fighting in three real boxing matches, two of which De Niro won. The two men also lived together during the preparation in order to develop the right kind of relationship and interaction. De Niro also spent a great deal of time getting to know the real Jake La Motta.

Because of good actors' hard work at getting to know their characters, there are few directors – however improvisatory or tied-down their style – who are not open to suggestions from their cast about things that might work better – different dialogue or actions, changes to the set or props,[21] even developments in the story. Screenwriters are always on set throughout the shoot so that they can modify the script as filming proceeds, which is one reason why published shooting scripts are often quite different from what appears on screen.

In the Cut: Editors

When the shooting is complete, it is the task of the editor, in collaboration with the director, to take the miles of celluloid[22] which have been produced in filming and create the final film. The good takes must be selected, and then shots taken from different angles must be cut up and rejoined to create scenes in such a way that we can make sense of what we are watching. Scenes which relate to the same idea may be assembled into a sequence (roughly equivalent to a chapter in a book), and the whole lot needs to be arranged in the right order. Then titles need to be included, dialogue and any sound effects need to be synchronised[23] and the musical score added. Walter Murch, the most celebrated film editor and sound mixer, says, 'My job as an editor is to gently prod the attention of the audience to look at various parts of the frame. And I do that by manipulating, by how and where I cut and what succession of images I work with.'[24] While *mise-en-scène* directs our attention to what goes into each shot, the way shots are connected together is, perhaps more than anything else, what gives film its unique power. The editing process takes individual shots and arranges them into a completed whole which tells a story and communicates a message. The editor's role in this is clearly vital. Murch says that editing, 'is not so much a *putting together* as it is a *discovery of a path*'.[25]

The classic Hollywood approach to editing – *continuity editing* – was to make it as seamless as possible. This does not mean that the completed film necessarily contains extremely long shots, but that the editing is subtle enough to keep the viewer focused on the action rather than being aware of the cuts. It whisks you through the narrative with each shot leading naturally into the subsequent one.

Everything follows in a smooth process of cause and effect, with no unexplained gaps of time or place. The fact that we do not notice just how many cuts there are in a film shows how this approach to editing works so well. *Finding Nemo* (Andrew Stanton, 2003), for example, contains just short of two thousand separate shots at an average length of 3·3 seconds, while *Dark City* (Alex Proyas, 1998) contains over three thousand at an average length of 1·8 seconds.[26]

Sometimes editors need to create more impact through their cuts. One common technique is cross-cutting, when the action alternates between two different scenes. It tends to be used when two events are taking place at the same time but which come to a single climax or resolution. A sequence shortly before the climax in *Silence of the Lambs* switches between the FBI who believe they have tracked down the house of the serial killer (Anthony Hopkins), and Clarice Starling (Jodie Foster) who is searching elsewhere. It builds significant tension because we know that Hannibal Lecter has a woman imprisoned in his basement who needs rescuing, and because the sequence builds certain expectations in the audience that are then thwarted. Perhaps the most famous example is the final sequence of *The Godfather* (Francis Ford Coppola, 1972) in which shots of the baptism of Michael Corleone's (Al Pacino) son are intercut with shots of Corleone's men assassinating rival heads of families. The stark contrast between Corleone saying, 'I renounce sin' and the brutal murders is extremely powerful.

Montage

Montage is a significant departure from continuity editing (though note that the word montage is also sometimes used to mean editing in general, especially in Europe). The term can describe rapid cutting between a number of scenes, often used as a device to condense the storytelling. *Ghostbusters* (Ivan Reitman, 1984), for example, parallels the Ghostbusters in action with a succession of newspaper headlines heralding their success. The use of montage to create a sense of excitement is now standard practice in music videos but it raised eyebrows among traditional film-makers when Richard Lester first popularised it with the Beatles films *A Hard Day's Night* (1964) and *Help!* (1965).

Montage can also describe the juxtaposition of shots to create new meaning – whether or not the director intends them to. The first person to demonstrate just how powerful this technique can be was Russian film-maker Lev Kuleshov. In 1918 he edited together some fragments of film which had already been shot including footage of famous actor Ivan Mozzhukhin. The same shot of Mozzhukhin's completely impassive face was alternated with images of a bowl of soup, a young girl playing and a woman in a coffin. The audience were amazed at his emotional range and depth, perceiving him to be reacting differently to each of the other images, though he was not in fact reacting to anything at all. Kuleshov's conclusion was that the meaning is created entirely by the juxtaposition. This had an enormous influence on film-makers in Russia (hence it is known as Soviet montage) – especially Vsevolod Pudovkin and Sergei Eisenstein whose work had a profound impact on film-makers around the world. Eisenstein believed that the aim of the juxtapositions was to create a visual shock,[27] graphically illustrated in the famous Odessa Steps sequence from *The Battleship Potemkin* (1925). Montage, in this broader sense of a juxtaposition (whether shocking or not) of shots which creates new meaning, at some level applies to any transition between scenes – even between successive shots.

All For One: Movies and Meaning

Those who are telling a story through a film have, therefore, five basic tools to work with: *mise-en-scène*, editing, the dialogue and the actors' performance, to which may be added the soundtrack (sound effects and musical score).[28] *Mise-en-scène* is to do with spatial factors within an individual frame; editing, dialogue, performance and soundtrack are to do with temporal factors (across several or all of the frames). Meaning is created in both spatial and temporal ways, as well as through the development of the plot (I will explore this further in the next chapter).

Indeed, every aspect of the film creates meaning, or plays a part in the creation of meaning for the film as a whole. Anything which works against the film's meaning is almost certain to have been spotted and expunged long before the final cut. Whether it is conveying emotion, developing character, furthering the narrative, making associations with other films or books or whatever, alerting us to hidden significance or drawing our attention to certain ideas, every element plays an important part in creating the whole. I am not suggesting that every last detail should be taken as evidence of a particular worldview. I am saying that as we learn more of how the director, screenwriter, actors and editors have exploited various techniques, it will help us to understand the film better. The more thought we give to aspects of the film, the richer our engagement with it, and the more insight our observations will have – even if others see things in different ways. And, after all, that is part of the fun of discussing films together.

The finished film is the product of a number of contributors bringing slightly – or sometimes very – different worldview perspectives to the project, but the film still communicates. It is important to realise that the concern here is not to reduce a film to a mere statement worldview. It is, first and foremost, a work of art. But all art communicates, reflecting the worldview of its creator(s). So whether the message is clear or somewhat distorted, if we want to engage with films at a worldview level, then we need to understand the techniques used to tell the story, as we have seen in this chapter. However, we must also understand how the narrative itself is put together and what that reveals to us about the world-views within it. We will consider this in the next chapter.

Notes

1 Oh, all right, I will. The gaffer is in charge of the electrical department which in the film world means lighting. His chief assistant is the best boy and his responsibilities might range from doing all the setting up in a small crew through to having significant management responsibilities for the team in a large crew. In the UK and Australia, the grips are responsible for the camera mounting – dollies (trucks enabling the camera to move), cranes, and so on. In North America, grips are also involved in the lighting, though are not responsible for the actual lights themselves. They sort out the rigging, erect shades, filters and so forth. The chief, or key, grip's main assistant is also called a best boy. Female best boys are usually called best girls on set, but are listed as best boys in the credits. All clear now?

2 *Crash* Trivia, IMDb.com – pro.imdb.com/title/tt0375679/ trivia.

3 Philippa Boyens worked with Jackson on all three films; Stephen Sinclair was involved only in *The Two Towers* (2002). Walsh, Boyens and Jackson won the Oscar for Best Adapted Screenplay for *The Return of the King* in 2003.

4 J.R.R. Tolkien's *The Lord of the Rings* has many very dedicated fans, some of whom felt that Jackson's team had not been faithful enough to the original. My own perspective – as a long-time fan of the books – was that Jackson had succeeded remarkably well in bringing the story to the screen, though with a small number of disappointing changes. Some of the DVD extras gave the film-makers' justification for why these changes had been made.

5 At the time of writing, filming is in progress and the film is scheduled to be released in late 2007.

6 Tristan Deveney, 'Chris Weitz Interview', *BridgeToTheStars.net*, 2004 – www.bridgetothestars.net/ index.php?p=weitzinterview.

7 Roger Michell interviewed by Adrian Hennigan, BBC.co.uk –www.bbc.co.uk/films/2004/11/25/roger_michell_endur ing_love_interview.shtml.

8 Selznick produced *King Kong* (Merian C. Cooper and Ernest B. Schoedsack, 1933), *Gone with the Wind* (Victor Fleming, 1939) and over seventy other films, mostly in the thirties and forties.

9 Thalberg produced around ninety films in the twenties and thirties, including *Tarzan the Ape Man* (W.S. Van Dyke, 1932), *A Night at the Opera* (Sam Wood, 1935) and *A Day at the Races* (Sam Wood, 1937), although he rarely featured in the credits.

10 Quoted in Geoffrey Macnab, *Key Moments in Cinema: The History of Film and Film-makers* (London: Hamlyn, 2001) p. 20–21.

11 François Truffaut, 'Une Certaine Tendance du Cinéma Français' in *Cahiers du Cinéma*, No. 31, January 1954. It was in this essay that Truffaut coined the term *politique des auteurs*, now more usually known as 'auteur theory' thanks

to Andrew Sarris's 1962 essay, 'Notes on the Auteur Theory'.

12 A key influence on this shift was Roland Barthes' 1968 essay 'The Death of the Author' which can be found in his *Image, Music, Text*, trans. Stephen Heath (London: Fontana, 1993), first published in 1977.

13 See William Beard, *The Artist as Monster: The Films of David Cronenberg* (Toronto: University of Toronto Press, 2005).

14 See Foster Hirsch, *Love, Sex, Death and the Meaning of Life: The Films of Woody Allen*, second edition (Cambridge, Mass.: Da Capo, 2001).

15 See Eddie Robson, *Coen Brothers* (London: Virgin, 2003).

16 Sidney Lumet, *Making Movies* (New York: Vintage, 1995) p. 10.

17 Roger Michell in Adrian Hennigan, 'Getting Direct with Directors . . . No. 5: Roger Michell', *BBC Movies – Calling the Shots* – www.bbc.co.uk/films/callingtheshots/roger_michell.shtml.

18 Ed Harris, 'Acts Of Violence' featurette on *A History of Violence* DVD (Entertainment in Video, 2006).

19 Julie Delpy 'Under Kieslowski's Microscope', DVD featurette on *Three Colours: White,* disc 2 of *The Three Colours Trilogy* (Artificial Eye, 2004).

20 Method acting describes a range of approaches to achieving authenticity in acting. 'The Method' tends to be used to refer to the approach famously taught by Lee Strasberg in the 1940s and 50s, inspired by the Stanislavski system developed by Russian theatre director Konstantin Stanislavski. Strasberg, who focused on emotional memories, taught Paul Newman, Al Pacino, Jane Fonda and many other great actors. Two other great exponents, though with different emphases from Strasberg, were Sanford Meisner (whose students include Robert Duvall, Diane Keaton, and Steve McQueen) and Stella Adler (a former student of Stanislavski whose own students include Marlon Brando and Robert De Niro).

21 David Cronenberg relates that, while filming *A History of*

Violence, Viggo Mortensen would frequently return from weekends at home with items that he had bought specifically to be props for his character ('Acts Of Violence' featurette on *A History of Violence* DVD).

22 And it is miles – an incredible 236 miles for *Apocalypse Now* (Francis Ford Coppola, 1979) of which just over 1% was used in the final movie. An average film creates something in the region of forty miles of raw footage, of which around 5% is used.

23 The sound is almost invariably recorded separately from the visual footage – often in studios after shooting on location.

24 Walter Murch in Michelle Norris, 'Behind the Scenes with Film Editor Walter Murch', *NPR* – www.npr.org/templates/story/story.php?storyId=4994411.

25 Walter Murch, *In the Blink of an Eye: A Perspective on Film Editing* (Beverly Hills, Calif.: Silman-James, 1995) p. 4.

26 The Average Shot Lengths are given by David Bordwell in *The Way Hollywood Tells It: Story and Style in Modern Movies* (Berkeley and Los Angeles: University of California Press, 2006) pp. 122–123.

27 The avant-garde techniques of these early Soviet film-makers were a rejection of the smooth, comfortable continuity editing of the capitalist west.

28 Walter Murch says, 'By manipulating what you hear and how you hear it – and what other things you do not hear – you can not only help tell the story, you can help the audience get into the mind of the character.' (Michelle Norris, 'Behind the Scenes with Film Editor Walter Murch.')

5. Telling Tales

The Narrative Structure of Films

Human beings have been telling stories since the beginning of our history. We have always told stories to explain the origins of natural phenomena and of ourselves. We tell stories about our communities and our own lives as part of the process of making sense of our history. Stories make connections between the past and present, and suggest what the future might hold, helping us to discern cause and effect. They make connections with the world around us so that we understand where we fit into it. They help us to discern relationships between things. In short, they enable us to make sense of our experiences and help us to see what meaning there might be in them. Philip Pullman says:

> Stories are vital. Stories never fail us because, as Isaac Bashevis Singer says, 'events never grow stale.' There's more wisdom in a story than in volumes of philosophy. . . . All stories teach, whether the storyteller intends them to or not. They teach the world we create. They teach the morality we live by. They teach it much more effectively than moral precepts and instructions.[1]

In other words, stories communicate worldviews. Brian Godawa writes:

> Every story is informed by a worldview. And so every movie, being a dramatic story, is also informed by a worldview. There is no such thing as a neutral story in which events and characters are presented objectively apart from interpretation. Every choice an author makes, from what kinds of characters she creates to which events she includes, is determined by the author's worldview. A worldview even defines what a character or event is for the writer – and therefore for the audience. And the worldview or philosophy of a film is conveyed much in the same way as stories of old would convey the values and beliefs of ancient societies – through dramatic incarnation of those values. In a sense, movies are the new myths of American culture.[2]

It is the story element which more often than not provides the biggest factor in our enjoyment of films. If a movie fails to deliver on that front, it is hard for other factors (the spectacle of action and effects, the depth of characterisation, the sharpness of the dialogue, and so on) to entirely make up for it.[3] If we want to be able to engage with mainstream narrative films at a worldview level, then we should learn to recognise how meaning is created through the storytelling. We need to look at how the narrative itself is structured and how the story is presented to us through images and sounds. The narratives of the majority of films have two fundamental features: First, they are about chains of events which are (mostly) linked by cause and effect. Second, they feature one or more central characters (protagonists) attempting to achieve some goal.

The Butterfly Effect

Films present a sequence of events: one thing causes another which causes another – maybe not immediately, but certainly before the film's conclusion. If the network of causes and effects fails to hold together and we become aware of plot holes, we easily become irritated. This is not to say that there cannot be coincidences, but that they should be reasonably justified if they are not to feel like holes. That is, coincidences are themselves the product of cause and effect which could, in principle, be known even if the film chooses not to spell them out. In *Tristan and Isolde* (Kevin Reynolds, 2006), during a fight with an Irish raiding party, Tristan (James Franco) is wounded by the poisoned blade of their leader Morholt. After defeating the Irish, Tristan's men believe him to be dead, put his comatose body into a boat and push it out to sea. The boat washes up on an Irish beach where Tristan is found and nursed back to health by Isolde (Sophie Myles), daughter of the Irish king – and Morholt's betrothed (which is how she can both recognise and treat the poison). It is this chance crossing of paths which makes their love both possible and doomed. While this is an amazing coincidence, it is not a denial of causality, but rather a twist of fate since tides and currents are subject to higher powers – Tristan and Isolde believe their love is meant to be. Some films, however, depart from classical narrative construction by deliberately relying on unjustifiable coincidences – the 'infinite improbability drive' in *The Hitchhiker's Guide to the Galaxy* (Garth

Jennings, 2005), for example. In such cases, it is important to ask what this tells us about the worldview of the film. In the case of *Hitchhiker's*, writer Douglas Adams[4] used absurdity to communicate the absence of any ultimate meaning of life in an entirely naturalistic universe.

Closely related to this, the fictional worlds created in films normally work in a consistent way. Any story which is set in the normal 'real world' of our experience[5] should have a consistent reality because it is subject to the same laws of physics as the world in which we live. But a story does not have to be realistic in order to be consistent. The world of Harry Potter is nothing like reality, but the magic works in a fully consistent way. When the fictional world is not consistent, we need to ask why. The inconsistency in the world of *The Matrix Trilogy* (the Wachowski Brothers, 1999, 2003) is something that has generated heated debate among fans: is it a result of careless plotting, or does it indicate another level of reality beyond the two we are explicitly shown?[6] The utterly inconsistent reality of *Being John Malkovich* (Spike Jonze, 1999) and the difficulty of distinguishing dreams from wakefulness in *The Science of Sleep* (Michel Gondry, 2006) are both profoundly influenced by postmodernism[7] and are intentional denials of conventional narrative.

Films may also play around with time. Most proceed in a linear fashion (we see events in the order they happen), although there may be flashbacks (or occasionally flash-forwards, as in Spike Lee's 2006 film *Inside Man*) to help us understand something that is happening in the present. Some, however, use a variety of devices which may break the linearity of the story. The central feature of *Memento* (Christopher Nolan, 2000) was the reversed telling of the story: we start the film knowing what happened and spend the rest of the time trying to unpick the chain of events which led to up to it. However, while it may be difficult to work out the causes and effects in *Memento*, it is important to us that they are there to be discovered somehow. *Eternal Sunshine of the Spotless Mind* (Michel Gondry, 2004) also tells much of the story backwards as the memories of Joel Barrish (Jim Carrey) are progressively wiped, beginning with the most recent. *Pulp Fiction* (Quentin Tarantino, 1994) famously featured a number of more or less related narratives linked in a discontinuous fashion. Tarantino did not randomly jumble the scenes, but arranged them on the basis of what he wanted to communicate, rather than being tied to a chronological order.

Note that these three areas of causality, consistency and time are all related to the question, 'What is reality?' – our first worldview question in Chapter 2 (page 32). It is important to also think about what else you can identify about the nature of reality as seen in the film, as we saw previously.

The Mission

The second fundamental feature of narratives is the focus on one or more central characters attempting to achieve some goal.[8] The hero wants something out of life, and the movie is the account of their progress towards attaining it. After analysing hundreds of movies (from the studio era as well as recent ones), Kristin Thompson concluded that, contrary to the three-act structure advocated in most screenwriting manuals,[9] they are nearly always structured into four major (and often carefully balanced) parts plus an epilogue.[10]

The first part, the Set-up, 'establishes the characters'

world, defines the main characters' purposes, and culminates in a turning point near the half-hour mark'.[11] It gives us what we need to follow the story, enabling us to identify with the protagonist and to understand what he or she is trying to achieve. Thompson refers to the second part as the Complicating Action. The Complicating Action may show the central character trying to achieve the goal in a different way, facing some challenge which changes the context in which the goal is pursued, or a modification in the goal itself. The emotions are rising more now and we re-evaluate some of the assumptions we have made in the Set-up. This section often ends around halfway through the film, almost always with some major event or big change. Third comes the Development in which 'the protagonist's struggle towards his or her goals typically occurs, often involving many incidents that create action, suspense and delay.'[12] Indeed, the delays are often such that he or she makes little headway towards achieving the goal. At the end of this section comes his or her lowest point when it looks as though the goal will never be reached. Part four is the Climax in which the protagonist succeeds (or fails), often with a twist in the tale. Finally, there is frequently an epilogue of some sort (which may be extremely short or very long as in *Return of the King* (Peter Jackson, 2003) where it serves as the epilogue for the entire trilogy) which 'confirms the stability of the situation, while settling subplots and tying up motifs'.[13]

Last Action Hero

Protagonists can be active or passive. Active protagonists have objectives which they deliberately pursue, and attention is focused on what action they take along the way. Robert McKee says:

> the protagonist is a wilful being . . . A protagonist's willpower may be less than that of the biblical Job, but powerful enough to sustain desire through conflict and ultimately take actions that create meaningful and irreversible change.[14]

Usually protagonists have two goals which are inter-connected in some way. It is common for one of these to be romantic, and success with this goal is dependent on succeeding with the other. There is frequently some time pressure on achieving the goals – an appointment, the end of a journey, an impending disaster, and so on. Some protagonists, however, are passive, reacting to the world around them without any internal compulsion or any goals which they proactively pursue. Chance the gardener (Peter Sellers) in *Being There* (Hal Ashby, 1979) is a classic example. A passive protagonist does not make for an obvious hero, and can often be an anti-hero. Nevertheless, they commonly end up needing to reach a particular goal – otherwise there is no narrative tension. McKee says that, 'A story cannot be told about a protagonist who doesn't want anything, who cannot make decisions, whose actions effect no change at any level.'[15] A passive protagonist's goals tend to be internal (mental, psychological or emotional) rather than external, and to be free from time restraints. The Dude (Jeff Bridges) in *The Big Lebowski* (Joel Coen, 1998) is a slacker who wants to do nothing more than chill out, though once he is mistaken for a millionaire with the same surname he becomes active in trying to return to his slacker lifestyle. Multiple protagonists with interwoven storylines have become more common, though they have been significant since *Grand Hotel* (Edmund Goulding, 1932). *L.A. Confidential* (Curtis Hanson, 1997) has three equally important protagonists and *Closer* (Mike Nichols, 2004) has four, while Robert Altman's *Short Cuts* (1993) and *Gosford Park* (2001) have large collections of characters, with no central figure whose story is being told. Other examples of ensemble films include *Magnolia* (Paul Thomas Anderson, 1999), *Amores Perros* (Alejandro González Iñárritu, 2000) and *Love Actually* (Richard Curtis, 2003). The effect of having multiple protagonists is to diminish the focus on any single character, which has the potential to weaken the story. It takes a good screenwriter to pull it off well, and the various strands need to be clearly linked (by characters, location or theme) if we are to make sense of the film.[16] For convenience, I shall continue to refer to single protagonists in this chapter, but it all applies to two or more protagonists.

Enemy At The Gates

Protagonists cannot be heroes in a vacuum (unless they are astronauts). Films need some kind of tension in the narrative to propel it forwards – some antagonism. Robert McKee states that: 'A protagonist and his story can only be as intellectually fascinating and emotionally compelling as the forces of antagonism make them.'[17] This usually comes through obstacles or opposition standing in the way of the protagonist achieving the desired goal. At the simplest level, the hero has an adversary to fight (such as Bond villains), but the difficulties could result from something impersonal such as forces of nature (ice in *The Day After Tomorrow* (Roland

Emmerich, 2004) and *Eight Below* (Frank Marshall, 2006) for example). Many protagonists face internal as well as external conflict, of course. Passive protagonists are usually struggling primarily with internal conflict. In *About Schmidt* (Alexander Payne, 2002), Warren Schmidt (Jack Nicholson) sets off in a camper van to visit his daughter Jeannie (Hope Davies) and help her prepare for her wedding. However, Jeannie resents his constant attempts to control her life and insists that he arrive no earlier than the day before. Schmidt experiences external conflict (with Jeannie, her fiancé and his family) but primarily the story is about him struggling with the kind of person he is and what his life adds up to. On the other hand, a film which has no room for the internal struggles of the characters may be fun, but it lacks depth *(The Da Vinci Code* (Ron Howard, 2006) for example). Unless characters are flat, two-dimensional figures, we will be aware of some of their personal journey of self-discovery, though the focus of most films is on the external conflict more than the internal.

These two opposing forces – the protagonist and the obstacles in his or her way – are key ways in which the worldview of the film is communicated. The protagonist represents – and perhaps even expresses – a particular worldview. It is often the case that the protagonist represents the worldview of the writer – especially if the film endorses (and encourages us to endorse) the protagonist's worldview. After all, a writer is unlikely to want us to side with a character he or she disagrees with. By the same token, the antagonistic forces are likely to represent worldviews for which the writer feels some antipathy. In *Collateral* (Michael Mann, 2004), hit-man Vincent (Tom Cruise) justifies his actions by espousing an atheistic worldview. Though taxi-driver protagonist Max

(Jamie Foxx) does not explicitly deny this view, he clearly thinks that Vincent's nihilism is morally defective. As we think about these opposing forces from a worldview perspective, we need first to identify the protagonist's goals. What do these goals suggest about how the central characters view life? As we try to identify answers to our five worldview questions, we need to pay attention to what the protagonist thinks of the world around them, how they interact with other characters and their community, how they respond to the forces of antagonism, how they know what they know, how they make decisions (especially moral ones), what values they have, and what they think human beings most need. Of course, if the antagonistic forces are personal beings, then all these questions can be asked of them too. Not all of these will be clear in every film, but they are vital clues to look for. Sometimes we will not even need to search for them since characters may make some speech or declaration setting out their perspectives, motives and reasons. The classic (and much parodied) example of this is the Bond villain who, on the point of achieving victory and destroying 007, recklessly stops to justify his or her actions.

What's My Motivation?

Motivation is not just something that relates to the actions of the characters, though. There tends to be some motivation, some reason, for everything in most films – including the natures of the various characters. Almost as soon as a character appears, we make deductions about what kind of people they are from what they say or do, from what is said about them, or from their appearance and demeanour. It is interesting that, while the protagonist may be on a journey of self-discovery, the nature of most other characters usually stays the same throughout the film. When characters do change their attitudes or behaviour there is a reason for it – and we need to pay close attention to what it is.

There also needs to be some motivation for every event – that is if the film's reality is consistent and events are linked by cause and effect. Random events are unsatisfying to viewers unless the movie is questioning reality or causality, and even then are often very unsettling. Thompson writes: 'Unity and clarity demand that everything in the film should be motivated whether in advance or in retrospect; that is, each event, object, character trait and other narrative component should be justified, explicitly or implicitly, by other elements in the film.'[18] There are exceptions, naturally. We get no motivation for the repeating day experienced by Phil (Bill Murray) in *Groundhog Day* (Harold Ramis, 1993), for example. We assume it must have been the result of some supernatural intervention, but it is never spelled out for us. Motivation for events often comes from the individual characters in the film and what kind of people they are. It may also arise from politics (Deep Throat's contact with journalists Bob Woodward (Robert Redford) and Carl Bernstein (Dustin Hoffman) during the Watergate scandal in *All the President's Men* (Alan Pakula, 1976), for example); economics (in *Glengarry Glen Ross* (James Foley, 1992), the motivation for the desperate actions of four real estate agents is that their jobs are on the line); warfare or countless other large-scale human actions. Motivation can also come from the physical circumstances – sickness *(Awakenings*, Penny Marshall, 1990), weather *(The Perfect Storm,* Wolfgang Peterson,

2000), natural disasters (*Deep Impact,* Mimi Leder, 1998) or all kinds of other things. In other words, we need to be constantly asking: Why is this happening? Why do the characters do and say these particular things?

Changing Lanes

It is vital to notice what changes take place as a result of the various motivating factors. What happens as a result of a particular event? What happens to the protagonist and other characters? We may see change take place externally – in what characters do or say – but this is evidence for some internal change – in what they think, believe or value. By the end of *Groundhog Day* we see that the way Phil speaks to people and acts towards them is radically different from how he was initially. He has moved, from cynicism and selfishness, through despair to become self-giving and self-effacing – clear evidence of a deep change within. As we saw in Chapter 2, apart from instinctive responses, everything people do is a consequence of their worldview. So when we observe change in a character's behaviour it may give us vital clues as to how their worldview – or the writer's worldview – is shaping that behaviour and driving their actions. Thompson's identification of four major parts in many films was based on tracing shifts in the protagonist's goals – in the tactics used to attain the goal, in the circumstances facing the protagonist, or in what the goal really is. Of these, a shift in the goal itself is likely to be particularly revealing of the underlying worldview. Changes which occur (like all actions and events) will normally have some motivation or justification behind them. The key question, then, is 'Why has this happened?'

Changes have consequences – the chain of causes and events continues – so we need to be alert to what they are. In the fictional world of a film, the consequences of actions and events are deliberately chosen by the writer, perhaps for maximum impact, or to make a certain point. Again, we must ask why, and what this reveals about the worldview. Many movies have something – a line of dialogue, a character, an object or image, a gesture, and many other possibilities – early in the story which foreshadows key plot development which will come later on. Spike Lee's *Inside Man* opens with a voiceover from Dalton Russell (Clive Owen) in which he says, 'Pay strict attention to what I say because I choose my words carefully and never repeat myself. . . . The Where can most readily be described as a prison cell. But there is a vast difference from being stuck in a tiny cell and being in prison.' The injunction to 'pay attention' explicitly primes us to watch out for the significance of his words. It remains a 'dangling cause' until the climax of the film when, ironically, the words are repeated just as we are puzzling over how he has perpetrated an apparently perfect crime. In *The Sixth Sense* (M. Night Shyamalan, 1999) Dr Malcolm Crowe (Bruce Willis) has significant problems in his marriage, with a distinct lack of communication. This becomes powerfully significant at the end of the film, although viewers tend to misinterpret it at first – as well as being a foreshadowing it is also a red herring. It is probably impossible to keep track of everything we see and hear in a film in order to spot the future consequences, though filmmakers have many ways of drawing our attention to the key things. Nevertheless, what this does suggest is that we need to watch films very actively.

The Final Reel

As we pay attention to change and consequences, we will obviously consider the resolution of the narrative. But it warrants particular attention because this is the point at which the writer and director are bringing everything to a head, rounding it all off, tying up loose ends (or not), creating the final emotional mood which viewers will take with them as they leave the cinema, and underscoring the message in other ways. What does the ending tell us about the film's message? The first thing to consider is the central aspect of most films: how are things different for the protagonist at the end of the film compared to the beginning? Usually some significant change has occurred by the conclusion of the film – generally, though not always, to make the world a better place, at least for the protagonist. The short epilogue at the end of many films provides a brief opportunity to show the new state of affairs, and perhaps to resolve a sub-plot.

In a few stories, however, no real change happens and life carries on as before – which in itself may be a comment on the nature of reality. Andrew Niccol's extremely thought-provoking *Lord of War* (2005) was particularly powerful because Niccol refused to resolve the narrative in the way we hoped. Nicholas Cage plays Yuri, an arms dealer who is challenged about the morality of his trade yet continues with it. We need to ask why nothing has changed and what the film-makers want to communicate through this.

Even when there has been no substantial external change, the protagonist has usually still had *some* character arc: he or she has been on a personal journey of at least some self-discovery – even if it has taken him or her back to the same place. Yuri has been through a process of questioning his life but is finally confirmed in his opinion that there are no moral absolutes and that he is doing the right thing (for him). We also need to ask, therefore, what does the central character discover about himself or herself during the course of the film?

We must also reflect on whether or not the film ends in the way we expected. Of course, the film finishes in whatever way the film-makers want it to – from their perspective it is the correct ending. The question is, why does it end *this* way, as opposed to other ways in which it could have ended? But the correct ending is not necessarily what we are prepared for. What matters here is not our predilection for happy or sad endings, but whether the ending is appropriate within the framework established by the film itself. For example, does it end in failure or disappointment for the protagonist when we have come to expect success or happiness? The lack of redemptive resolution in *Lord of War* is profoundly disturbing; the emotional climax is not at all what we wanted or expected – and the film packs a bigger punch as a result. Whether the ending conforms to our expectations or not, we need to assess how the beliefs, values and attitudes we have seen in the film are ultimately reinforced or undercut by the ending. These are key indicators of the worldview. Another way of expressing it is, what does this movie ultimately suggest about how we should or should not live?

Finally, it is important to identify whether the ending of the film is closed or open. With a closed ending the problem has been resolved, the questions have been answered and emotions have been satisfied. An open ending does not necessarily tie up all the loose ends, satisfactorily answer every question or generate the appropriate emotional finale. Instead, there may be a lingering doubt about the state of affairs at the end of the film, or some uncertainty over a main character's motives, or perhaps the resolution is emotionally unsatisfying in some way *(Lost in Translation* (Sofia Coppola, 2003) and *Broken Flowers* (Jim Jarmusch, 2005), both starring Bill Murray, are good examples). Endings cannot be completely open, however: they need to work reasonably well or people are unlikely to enjoy the film at all.

Theme Park

It is all very well to analyse the narrative in this way, but we must make sure that we also give some thought to what the film is actually about. The protagonist has a goal and things happen for particular reasons, but what is the *theme?* It may be that the protagonist's goal coincides with the real theme of the film, but it does not always. In *Amadeus* (Milos Forman, 1984), the goals of Salieri (F. Murray Abraham) are to destroy Mozart (Tom Hulce) and to achieve 'immortality' as a composer. But the film is about much more profound issues: Salieri is angry with God for giving greater musical genius to the unworthy Mozart than to himself, and he therefore sees his attack on Mozart as an attack on God. Deeper still, *Amadeus* is a reflection on forgiveness: Mozart recognises its importance both in his own life and in the opera we see him working on *(Le Nozze di Figaro);* whereas the hypocritical Salieri, who once saw himself as faithful to God, rejects it. In Chapter 1 I noted that virtually all films explore one or more of a handful of major themes: identity, morality, power, religion/spirituality, sexuality, happiness, freedom, love, reality and human nature. It is far from being a comprehensive list, and they are rather broad categories which can often be expressed in quite different ways. We could talk about fulfilment rather than happiness, or politics rather than power, and so on. But it is a useful list of themes which I am looking out for whenever I watch a movie. *Amadeus* has something to say about all of them in some way or other, though most films will only touch on some.

Films draw these themes to our attention in a number of ways, including the aspects of the narrative that we have considered already in this chapter. Motivation is a particularly key aspect to consider, as this is likely to be linked very closely to the themes which the film-makers most want to explore. So too is the resolution – after all, the director and screenwriter generally want us to take a particular perspective away from the film. The techniques of *mise-en-scène* and montage, which we discussed in the previous chapter, also play a vital role in alerting us to the themes – they can both provide indicators of significance. Lighting, colour, camera angle and the use of tracking or zoom shots, and a raft of other techniques can all direct our attention to particular elements of the scene, whether in an understated way or very straightforwardly, and so reinforce the importance of what we are seeing or hearing. Thinking about whose point of view we are seeing things from at a particular moment can also be important. Are we seeing things from the protagonist's perspective or that of another character? Or are we simply in the place of onlookers, perhaps seeing with something approaching omniscience?

Signs

Images in films can create meaning in two ways – they can be *denotative* or *connotative*. The denotative meaning is the obvious, surface level meaning. An on-screen image of a punch denotes exactly what it shows, even though we know that one actor has not really hit the other. The connotative meaning arises because images represent other things – they are symbols or signs which represent other things to us. A trail of clothes on the floor of a room usually indicates that a sexual encounter has occurred, for example. *Back to the Future* (Robert Zemeckis, 1985) starts with the camera moving around a room with many clocks. It denotes a room full of clocks, but the obvious connotation of clocks is time. The number of clocks and the variety of ages and styles adds a further connotation: the person who owns these clocks is a collector, quite probably an eccentric one. Even the weather in a scene can function in this way as an indicator of significance. When Justine (Jennifer Aniston) reaches a crucial point of decision in her life in *The Good Girl* (Miguel Arteta, 2002), the rain is coming down in torrents – but the film is set in Texas. Did the film-makers have no choice but to shoot in the rain (in which case the meaning is purely denotative – it means it was raining) or was it a deliberate way of layering more significance into the scene (it has obvious connotations of gloom or sadness, and since it marks a change from the prevailing sunshine in the film, it also has the additional connotation of being unsettled)? The film music also serves a crucial function in creating connotative meaning. It provides the right emotional context to the scene and can profoundly influence how we read what we see on screen.

One very important indicator of significance arising from *mise-en-scène* is the presence of motifs – repeated lines, concepts, metaphors, images or perhaps music. *Serendipity* (Peter Chelsom, 2001) features recurring gloves, a five-dollar bill and an ice rink, and repeatedly references *Cool Hand Luke* (Stuart Rosenberg, 1967) and Gabriel García Márquez's novel *Love in the Time of Cholera*. The lovers see these things as confirmations that fate intends them to be together. The title of the film already suggests what the central theme might be, but the motifs establish it further as an exploration of luck versus fate. One of the most overdone uses of motifs I recall seeing was in *Sirens* (John Duigan, 1994) which used the recurring images of snakes and shipwrecks to ensure that we picked up the themes of temptation and disintegrating lives. The Blue Fairy from the story of Pinocchio is a prominent motif in *AI: Artificial Intelligence* (Steven Spielberg, 2001) – it represents a misplaced hope which nevertheless provides a reason for living.

Montage can also be a potent indicator of significance through juxtaposing two shots which may reflect or contrast each other in important ways. One famous example of this is the match cut (two scenes linked by a repeated – or apparently continuing – action, shape or *mise-en-scène*) in Stanley Kubrick's *2001: A Space Odyssey* (1968). It cuts from a prehistoric bone spinning in the air to a revolving space station, neatly encompassing human evolution from the first use of tools through to the development of machines which enable us to leave Earth far behind.

The purpose of looking carefully for these indicators of significance – and of paying conscious attention to the various elements of structure we discussed earlier in the chapter – is not to collect trivia or to play intellectual games (though of course it is great fun as well). Rather it is to help us identify the core themes of the film, to help us better understand its message and to see how the film-makers have emphasised various facets of the story to help ensure that the message hits home. As we become more proficient at understanding how a film is structured, we also get better at seeing how it communicates at a worldview level.

Notes

1 Philip Pullman, Carnegie Medal acceptance speech.
2 Brian Godawa, *Hollywood Worldviews: Watching Films with Wisdom and Discernment* (Downers Grove, Ill.: IVP, 2002) p. 25. Stories that explain some fundamental aspect of life are called myths. The word myth in this technical sense does not imply that the story is untrue, but that it functions as an explanation. Some are true; some are not, functioning perhaps as metaphors. The account of creation in Genesis 1 can properly be called myth whether or not we believe that the timescale of events described is literal or in some sense metaphorical or even completely untrue. Regardless of timescales, its *primary* purpose is to explain that God is the creator and that we are made in his image – it is a story of meaning. When Richard Dawkins says, 'I believe that all life, all intelligence, all creativity and all "design" anywhere in the universe, is the direct or indirect product of Darwinian natural selection,' (*Edge: The World Question Center*, 2005 – www.edge.org/q2005/q05_easyprint.html#dawkins) it is equally a myth, regardless of whether his belief is true or not. They are both explanatory stories. Myths are, therefore, the most important stories that we tell, and movies that have mythic elements are often some of the most powerful we encounter. *The Lord of the Rings* and the *Star Wars* cycle are both strongly mythic. However, stories

do not need to be mythic to be important.

3 Of course, we may watch a musical or a special-effects blockbuster *primarily* for something other than the storyline, though the narrative is still an essential part of the whole. It is also the case that there are films which are non-narrative, instead combining images and sounds in an abstract way to create a certain kind of aesthetic experience (*Koyaanisqatsi* (Godfrey Reggio, 1982) is a powerful example), but then we tend to infer the stories behind the images we see as well as bring our own stories to bear on our experience of the film.

4 Adams wrote the original story for BBC Radio as well as all its many subsequent variants, all of which changed aspects of the story. Adams was also responsible for all the changes in the film version of the story, although he died while writing the screenplay, which was then completed by Karey Kirkpatrick.

5 Bear in mind that the reality within every film is invented at *some* level. Even a film of true events is a reconstruction of those events, not the events themselves. A documentary gets closer to reality, but the way the subject matter is presented is still controlled by the film-makers.

6 The inconsistency arises because Neo is able to perform some superhuman feats in the world of Zion and the machines – the world which is presented to us as the real world. For more on this see my chapter 'This is the Construct: Postmodernism and *The Matrix*' in Steve Couch (ed.) *Matrix Revelations: A Thinking Fan's Guide to the Matrix trilogy* (Milton Keynes: Damaris, 2003) pp. 97–119.

7 See Chapter 3 for a summary of postmodernism.

8 Some writers on film are very influenced by the ideas of Joseph Campbell (1904–1987), a writer on mythology and comparative religion who claimed that all stories about heroes contain the same features and patterns. He expressed this as the monomyth – the archetypal hero myth which underlies all mythic tales – in his 1949 book *The Hero with a Thousand Faces* (New York: Pantheon Books, 1949).

Although this is the book for which Campbell is famous, his ideas reached a very wide audience through George Lucas. Lucas was making little progress with the story for *Star Wars* until he read Campbell's book and modelled the story on the ideas in it. Campbell himself became better known through the American Public Broadcasting Service (PBS) series *The Power of Myth*, first broadcast in 1988, the year after Campbell's death. Campbell's ideas have more recently been popularised by Christopher Vogler in *The Writer's Journey* (London: Pan, 1999). First published in 1992, it began life as a seven-page memo to Hollywood studios. Also of interest is Stuart Voytilla, *Myth and the Movies: Discovering the Mythic Structure of Over 50 Unforgettable Films* (Studio City, Calif.: Michael Wiese Productions, 1999).

9 For example, Robert McKee, *Story: Substance, Structure, Style, and the Principles of Scriptwriting* (London: Methuen, 1999).

10 Kristin Thompson, *Storytelling in the New Hollywood: Understanding Classical Narrative Technique* (Cambridge, Mass.: Harvard University Press, 1999) pp. 29–35.

11 David Bordwell, *The Way Hollywood Tells It: Story and Style in Modern Movies* (Berkeley and Los Angeles: University of California Press, 2006) p. 36.

12 Thompson, *Storytelling in the New Hollywood*, p. 28.

13 Bordwell, *The Way Hollywood Tells It*, p. 38.

14 McKee, *Story*, p. 137.

15 McKee, *Story*, p. 138.

16 Bordwell, *The Way Hollywood Tells It*, pp. 96–103.

17 McKee, *Story*, p. 317.

18 Thompson, *Storytelling in the New Hollywood*, p. 13.

6. Bending the Rules

Genres and Worldviews

Why do you choose to see a particular movie? The stars are certainly a big factor, though for most viewers probably not the biggest. We may decide to see a film because of the director or screenwriter. Something from, say, Andrew Niccol or the Coen Brothers is likely to deal with some big issues in an interesting way. But this tends to be more the approach of the cinephile or film buff. For most filmgoers, the key factor in selecting what to watch is usually the film's *genre*: what kind of movie it is. It is why video shops generally organise their stock by genre. Romantic comedies are a must for some people; for others horror has the same draw. My wife prefers crime thrillers; my first choice would tend to be 'arty' films.

Genre films are often derided as being formulaic and forgettable. They certainly can be (sequels seem especially prone to this blight), but it is rather unfair to write off *The Sound of Music* (Robert Wise, 1965) as 'just another musical' or *The Godfather* (Francis Ford Coppola, 1972) as 'just another gangster movie'. In fact, there seems to be some relationship between popularity and status. Some critics, who like to think of themselves as sophisticated, sneer at blockbusters whereas they will commend a minority-interest art film for its intelligence (while other reviewers are equally biased in the reverse direction). But as José Arroyo notes, 'just because the plot is simple doesn't mean the movie is – or that it doesn't offer complex pleasures'.[1]

However, as soon as we start to talk about genres, we run into difficulties. They are very hard to define. We usually know a science fiction film when we see one, but it is rather harder to pin down precisely what constitutes science fiction as opposed to fantasy or a science-based drama. *Eternal Sunshine of the Spotless Mind* (Michel Gondry, 2004) features imaginary technology that allows the wiping of specific memories, so does that make it science fiction? It certainly doesn't feel like it. Musicals are fairly obvious (though some films, like *The Fabulous Baker Boys* (Steve Kloves, 1989), include songs without being musicals); thrillers are much less so. Today's audiences expect scarier scares and gorier violence than in the fifties, so would Hitchcock's *Vertigo* (1958) or *North by Northwest* (1959) be considered thrillers if they were made today? What do we do with the fact that genres change over time?[2] Genres often overlap and individual films frequently combine aspects from various genres, so is it actually useful to apply such labels to movies anyway?

Arguably, genre labels are a convenient way to help the potential audience and a film's publicity people to put it into the appropriate pigeon-hole. They give moviegoers some degree of confidence about what they are going to watch. Identifying the genre creates the right expectations in people's minds. Sometimes a movie can be misunderstood because the wrong genre expectations are created. An example of this is *The Weather Man* (Gore

Verbinski, 2005) which the marketing people seemed to think was a comedy. One colleague expected a light, feel-good movie and was surprised to find that it was a serious drama, albeit one with some mildly amusing moments.

The Function of Genres

However, the idea of genre has more value than for simply categorising movies. A key question is how genre affects the way we respond to the films. Leo Braudy notes that, 'genre films forge a deliberate connection between each new instance of the genre and its past tradition and manifestations.'[3] A genre may be characterised by certain recurring plot elements (as with murder mysteries) or by visual elements (the high contrast and dark shadows of film noir, for example), settings (gangster films are set in cities; Westerns in open country) or themes (romantic comedies, for instance). David Bordwell and Kristin Thompson summarise the importance of genre conventions:

> By knowing conventions, the viewer has a pathway into the film. Such landmarks allow the genre movie to communicate information quickly and economically. When we see the weak sheriff, we strongly suspect that he will not stand up to the gunslinger. We can then focus attention on the cowboy hero as he gets slowly drawn into helping the townspeople defend themselves.[4]

Genres set up certain expectations in us because we are so familiar with the conventions (often subconsciously).[5]

If we are expecting a murder mystery, we are alert for clues from the outset, adopting an attitude of suspicion to everyone except (usually) the investigator. Conventions may lead us to expect those on the wrong side of the law to meet justice or death (*In the Heat of the Night* (Norman Jewison, 1967) for example) or alternatively to expect them to get away with it (as in Steven Soderbergh's 2001 movie *Ocean's Eleven*). We intuitively know which characters we are to identify with – and therefore whether the 'goodies' or the 'baddies' are likely to come out on top. But films can deliberately exploit these expectations to deliver a big surprise at the end, as in *Arlington Road* (Mark Pellington, 1999). Musical conventions within most genres play a very significant part in how we respond – think of the shrieking violins in the shower scene in *Psycho* (Alfred Hitchcock, 1960).

Being aware of genre conventions raises two important implications for thinking about worldviews and film. First, we discover that conventions sometimes help to establish a prevailing worldview within that genre. For example, the prevalence of sophisticated technology in much science fiction tends to emphasise human ingenuity and the adequacy of material solutions to all problems. Consequently, science fiction frequently expresses a rationalist or naturalist worldview. On the other hand, a common feature of horror is the existence of evil spiritual beings. The struggle against these evil forces is finely balanced; although their defeat is certain in that the story will have a positive resolution, there is nothing inherent in the fictional worlds themselves which makes this victory inevitable.[6] The prevailing worldview, then, is not materialist, but dualist – good and evil are equal and opposite forces. The worldview may even be one of the conventions – film noir is usually based on existentialist foundations. So being aware of the genre conventions enables us to see how the various elements are used to reinforce the standard perspectives.

Second, we can see how directors ignore, subvert or challenge those conventions. That focuses us on what message *this* film is communicating, distinct from that of other examples of the genre. While a genre may have a prevailing worldview, that is not to say that every film within the genre communicates the same worldview. Divergence from the conventions may well be a very significant clue to the worldview of an individual film. As I have indicated several times in this book, we need to be alert as viewers, questioning what we see to tease out the significance.

Genres Reloaded

The popularity of genres changes over time. Musicals, Westerns and gangster movies (once Hollywood staples) are not made nearly as often now as in their heyday. Teen comedies are a relatively recent development – a reflection of the increased spending power of that age-group. When we think of disaster movies, we tend to think primarily of the seventies (though there are plenty of examples from other decades); when future critics think of movies based on comic books, they will perhaps tend to think of the nineties and 'noughties'. These shifts in popularity are closely linked with the changes in worldview. Bordwell and Thompson write:

> Many film scholars believe that genres are ritualized dramas resembling holiday celebrations – ceremonies which are satisfying because they

reaffirm cultural values with little variation. . . . Some scholars would argue that genres go further and actually exploit ambivalent social values and attitudes. The gangster film, for instance, makes it possible for audiences to relish the mobster's swaggering freedom while still feeling satisfied when he receives his punishment. Seen from this standpoint, genre conventions arouse emotion by touching upon deep social uncertainties but then channel those emotions into approved attitudes.[7]

Given this strong connection between genres and the prevailing culture, it is perhaps not surprising that some of the most obvious genres have been extremely male-oriented, at least in the traditional forms exemplified by Hollywood in the modernist era. It is patently true in war movies. The context is obviously one of great violence perpetrated by men upon other men, and they tend to emphasise team loyalty and strong leadership – values often presented as male-oriented. Horror and science fiction have both also tended to be more tailored for a male audience. In the former case, this is perhaps because men enjoy opportunities to demonstrate their fortitude in the face of fear (perhaps the last vestiges of an instinctive response from the earliest days of humanity). Science fiction, by definition, imagines technology beyond anything we have currently and is almost inevitably dependent on special effects. These two aspects are often alienating to women (as are aliens themselves). Science fiction also frequently overlaps with other genres – especially war, horror and action – compounding the sense that a film is intended for testosterone-fuelled, geeky young men. The action movie is a more recent genre which in many ways subsumes both Westerns and gangster movies, but which even now often falls victim to the same gender imbalance. Other genres, of course, have a stronger appeal to women than to men – none more so than the romance. Musicals, which were hugely important during the Hollywood golden age, appealed more to women than men, though that is not to say that they had no appeal to men.[8]

There is not enough space here to adequately survey the interrelationship between worldviews and the development of various genres during the history of cinema, so I will focus briefly on just two which have been radically impacted by changing worldviews: the Western and the Romance.

Once Upon a Time in the Western

The Western occupied an important place in cinema almost from the start:[9] 'the bedrock of solid box office performance upon which the edifice of Hollywood economic dominance was built.'[10] In the thirties, the Western was confined to B-movies until John Ford revived its fortunes with *Stagecoach* (1939). It was his first Western for thirteen years, despite having established his career by making thirty-nine of them between 1917 and 1926. *Stagecoach* was marked by new levels of sophistication, depth of characterisation and by more significant themes (prejudice, greed, revenge, addiction and redemption). Its star, John Wayne, and location, Colorado's Monument Valley, were ever after inextricably associated with Ford.[11] Westerns cannot be defined rigidly, however. They are not simply stories of the frontier in the Old West (sometimes defined as the period from the American Civil War in 1860 to the closing of the

Frontier in 1890) since there are examples which are not set at the western frontier *(North to Alaska* (Henry Hathaway, 1960), for one) or which are not set during this period (Sam Peckinpah's *The Wild Bunch* (1969) is set in 1913, for example).

Much ink has been spilled over the Western genre because of the way it embodied certain values and themes. Westerns were mostly about fighting, conquest, guns, bows and arrows, the coming of the railroad and the telegraph, mastery over the environment and other stereotypically masculine themes. Their focus was on heroes who showed predominantly male characteristics of rugged independence, violence and justice – machismo.[12] Characteristically female concerns – family, community, love, nurturing and compassion – were secondary. James Monaco suggests that the Western was the most important genre in Hollywood because, 'it embodied so many of the myths – the frontier, individualism, the land, and law and order versus anarchy – upon which the national psyche of the United States still depends.'[13]

These values and themes reflect the dominant modernist context in which they were produced. It is no surprise that so many movie-makers gravitated towards the Western, nor that audiences were enthusiastic for the genre. At its core was that almost irrepressible modernist myth of progress – 'the onward march of civilization led by strong men and loyal women'.[14] Western rationalism, exemplified by tough, no-nonsense cowboy heroes, always prevailed over the 'primitive' pre-modern world of the Native Americans. In Ford's classic *The Searchers* (1956), Captain Clayton (Ward Bond) refers to the Indians as 'childish savages' – a perspective common to classic Westerns, though in later films it was a cause of shame.

Wild Wild West

By the sixties, with the rise in existentialism and the counterculture, many people were feeling that the straightforward morality of Westerns was irrelevant or plain wrong: 'Their themes were considered too traditional, too patriotic, even racist and sexist.'[15] Sergio Leone and Sam Peckinpah undercut audience expectations and 'redefined the genre's conception of heroism by revamping the stereotype of the "good bad man" into the just-barely-good bad man'.[16]

Leone's first Spaghetti Westerns – *A Fistful of Dollars* (1964), *For A Few Dollars More* (1965) and *The Good, the Bad and the Ugly* (1966) – are often hailed as the best Westerns ever. Leone's intention was to strip away the sentimentality which had characterised many Westerns: 'the cowboy picture has got lost in psychology . . . the west was made by violent, uncomplicated men, and it is this strength and simplicity that I try to recapture in my picture.'[17] 'Glamour, prettiness, historical sentimentality and moral preaching were out. Violence, ruthlessness, and materialist practicality were in. Leone added his own stylistic simplicity and dynamic visual sense.'[18] The combination of Clint Eastwood's taciturn anti-hero ('the man with no name'[19]), stunning cinematography which alternates long shots with extreme close-ups of boots, eyes, hands and guns as the tension builds to a gunfight, and Ennio Morricone's evocative scores, resulted in films which are as iconic as their star. Leone portrays American history as built on the exploits of grim, hard-hearted men who were motivated by greed and power – most pointedly in *Once Upon a Time in the West* (1968). It is arguably no more truthful a view of the Old West than that of the more sentimental earlier films, but it does present a counterbalancing perspective – one which in the sixties majestically challenged the modernist account of the spread of civilisation.

Peckinpah gave the Western an even harder edge. *The Wild Bunch* was the most graphically violent film to date, and in some ways helped to precipitate the decline in the genre:

> Its 'dirty' West . . . exploded the boundaries of the Western, making it very difficult for subsequent filmmakers to work in the genre because of the enormity of Peckinpah's accomplishment. How could one make a Western after *The Wild Bunch*? Many did, of course, but that film cast a shadow upon their work, a set of standards by which it would be measured and judged.[20]

However, he had a profound impact on subsequent makers of action movies. Lucien Ballard's beautiful wide-screen cinematography[21] together with Peckinpah's marrying of highly-choreographed, stylised violence and striking techniques made *The Wild Bunch* a landmark visually. Peckinpah coupled slow-motion with rapid montages of shots from different angles, particularly of figures who had been shot, emphasising the violence and intensity of the scene.[22] Slow-motion had been around for a long time, but Peckinpah's use of it in extremely violent scenes, inspired by Akira Kurosawa's films (e.g. *The Seven Samurai*, 1954), played a significant part in it becoming a tool for use in serious films.

The Wild Bunch is not only noteworthy for its violence and cinematography, however. Peckinpah situates his anti-heroes at a time when the Old West has all but disappeared.[23] A movie poster summarised their situation as, 'Unchanged men in a changing land. Out of step, out of place and desperately out of time.'[24] As the old, familiar world passes, a new, threatening one is dawning. Peckinpah underlines the demise of the old in a number of ways. He prefaces the first bloodbath of the film with a temperance society marching into what will imminently be the line of fire while singing 'As we gather at the river' – a hymn favoured by John Ford for funeral scenes in his traditional Westerns.[25] Outlaw leader Pike Bishop (William Holden) makes it clear several times that he believes in the old code of loyalty. He says, 'We're going to stick together, just like it used to be. When you side with a man, you stay with him. And if you can't do that, you're like some animal – you're finished! We're finished! All of us!' But Pike cannot keep to his code, having once abandoned his then partner Deke Thornton (Robert Ryan). Thornton was captured and is now the bounty hunter on Pike's trail, the reward being his freedom. Destruction looms over Pike and his gang – because of his mistakes and failures, and his growing inability to make good decisions.

The film may be set in 1913, but its message springs straight from the late sixties' worldview: old certainties have gone; former heroes have failed to live up to their principles, made mistakes and shown poor judgement; in their place come new uncertainties and anti-heroes. Oppressive forces must be overthrown, but otherwise just go with the flow. The sole surviving outlaw finally joins forces with Thornton and some revolutionary Mexicans, reflecting, 'It ain't like it used to be, but it'll do.'

New Gun in Town

These Westerns were not the first to present an alternative view of the Old West. *Broken Arrow* (Delmer Daves, 1950) was possibly the first to side with Native Americans, and Arthur Penn's *The Left-Handed Gun* (1958) presented Billy the Kid as a delinquent, suicidal rebel without a cause. But they are important indicators of how worldview changes impacted on the films which were made – and which in turn reinforced the change of worldview within popular culture. Later movies also debunked Western myths: Penn's *Little Big Man* (1970) challenged racist attitudes as well as satirising Wild Bill Hickock and portraying General Custer as a genocidal lunatic. Robert Altman accused another American hero of racism and commercialism in *Buffalo Bill and the Indians, or Sitting Bull's History Lesson* (1976). Eastwood made two Westerns every bit as tough and cynical as Leone's – *High Plains Drifter* (1973) and *Pale Rider* (1985) – and two which challenged the Western's conventions – *The Outlaw Josey Wales* (1976) and *Unforgiven* (1992).[26] *Unforgiven's* attitudes to race and gender, violence and goodness are significantly different from those in classic Westerns. Nobody is good in this film: Gene Hackman's law-upholding sheriff turns out to be a torturing murderer, and Eastwood's reformed gunslinger reverts to swearing, drinking and killing. But it is clear that this exacts a heavy price on a man's soul. Eastwood says, 'When you are a perpetrator of violence . . . you rob your soul as well as the person you are committing a violent act against.'[27] Kevin Costner's *Dances with Wolves* (1990) is as senti-mental as early Westerns – not about the passing of the frontier days, however, but about the destruction of Native American communities and their way of life.

Costner's character reflects on the Sioux's deep connection to their environment saying, 'The only word that came to mind was harmony.'

Such revisionist accounts of the Old West are sometimes dismissed for being motivated by political correctness. But revisionism can be about honestly correcting the imbalances of previous histories rather than spinning information to serve a particular agenda. It is vital to think about what is happening at the worldview level. From a Christian perspective, we should applaud movies which challenge the racist and sexist attitudes of many classic Westerns since all human beings are made in God's image. As General Howard (Basil Ruysdael) says of the Apaches in *Broken Arrow,* 'My Bible says nothing about the pigmentation of their skin.' It is also right that we should not have naïve, rose-tinted views of heroes who, though commendable in some respects, were deeply flawed in others. On the other hand, we need to ask whether, for example, Altman's portrayal of Buffalo Bill as racist is fair given that he advocated rights for Native Americans. At the same time, we should not fall into dismissing everything about classic Westerns from the modernist era. The heroes of those films may have been tough loners, but they were often men of integrity and honesty, motivated by justice not greed.[28]

Love Stories

Peter Fraser comments on the success of *Titanic* (James Cameron, 1997) despite the flat characterisation and 'laughable' dialogue: 'it somehow strangely works. The popularity of *Titanic* made fools of all of us know-it-all critics and academics who groaned at the schmaltzy story. It forced the question, *Why* are people drawn back to these same romantic formulas again and again?'[29] He seems to be implying that it is the romantic line of action which forms perhaps the most significant element of a film's appeal. And no wonder, really. The romance has been a central part of literature and theatre for centuries. Effects may wow us at the time, the enigmas of a puzzle film may keep us pondering, but the emotional impact of a powerful love story like *Brief Encounter* (David Lean, 1945) or *Before Sunrise* and *Before Sunset* (Richard Linklater, 1995, 2004) can live with us forever. Does any aspect of human life stir us up so much? We may all want to be happy, but most of us would happily shun wealth and power for the sake of love. We see it as the primary way of becoming fulfilled (though of course we would probably quite like wealth, power and the looks of a Hollywood star as well).

The romance, like the Western, has been a hugely important genre from the earliest days of cinema. Unlike the Western its appeal is undiminished, although there have been significant changes. It is a difficult genre to treat in isolation as it often overlaps with other genres – romantic subplots seem to be not far short of compulsory. Indeed, romance is very often more than mere subplot as David Bordwell notes:

> The classical film has at least two lines of action ... Almost invariably, one of these lines of action involves heterosexual romantic love. This is, of course, not startling news. Of the one hundred films in the [unbiased sample used for analysing the classical system], ninety-five involved romance in at least one line of action, while eighty-five made that the principal line of action. ... To win the love of a

man or woman becomes the goal of many characters in classical films.[30]

Writing about more recent movies, Fraser comments:

> . . . the popular romances I see also suggest that love is the supreme human experience. They suggest that love is meant to last forever and that there is one man for every woman. And they suggest that love overcomes great impediments because when two people fall in love, the arrangement has been made by powers above.[31]

Guys and Dolls

It is no surprise that in the period up to 1960 many of the love stories relied on very traditional plot structures (boy meets girl; various obstacles get in the way; love finally blossoms) and gender stereotypes. The expectations reinforced by classic Hollywood fare have been discussed at length by many writers, few more entertainingly than Jeanine Basinger who writes about doing her 'first serious research into [her] future life as a female person by going to the movies':

> . . . the movies of those years contained some highly contradictory information about the woman's life. For instance, although women seemed to feel that husbands were the most important thing in the world, men apparently were not to be trusted because they were always dying unexpectedly, getting fired, and running off with chorus girls. These movie women seemed to feel that it was

desperately important to be married, yet marriage was an economic disaster in which women had to start baking pies professionally or taking in washing. Women were supposed to be sexually desirable, knowing how to tempt and satisfy men, but they were also supposed to be innocent and pure. How was that going to work?[32]

Basinger makes the point that she and her friends were perfectly aware of the untruthful escapism of what they were seeing, but were nevertheless influenced by it – though not in the way envisaged by the film-makers:

The woman's film was successful because it worked out of a paradox. It both held women in social bondage and released them into a dream of potency and freedom. It drew women in with images of what was lacking in their own lives and sent them home reassured that their own lives were the right thing after all. If it is true, as many suggest, that Hollywood films repressed women and sought to teach them what they ought to do, then it is equally clear that, in order to achieve this, the movies first had to bring to life the opposite of their own morality. To convince women that marriage and motherhood were the right path, movies had to show women making the mistake of doing something else. By making the Other live on the screen, movies made it real. By making it real, they made it desirable. By making it desirable, they made it possible. They gave the Other substance, and thus gave it credibility. In asking the question, What should a woman do with her life? they created the possibility of an answer different from the one they intended to provide at the end of the movie.[33]

David Shumway also notes that classical Hollywood films end up almost subliminally communicating a subversive message:

> The specific illusion that the screwball comedy constructs is that one can have both complete desire and complete satisfaction and that the name for this state of affairs is marriage. But the other side of the romantic economy is that satisfaction is the death of desire. . . . romance seeks an idealized object, and when that object is attained, love ceases to be romantic. Marriage must be the death of romance between the members of the couple, who, if they are to continue to participate in romance, must find other partners. Hence, for the project of the screwball comedy to work, romance must occur outside of marriage, and marriage must be the end of the movie.[34]

This is clearly the case in *His Girl Friday* (Howard Hawks, 1940). Hildy Johnson (Rosalind Russell) is about to marry and settle down to a quiet life as wife and mother. But when she tells her former husband and boss, newspaper editor Walter Burns (Cary Grant), he does everything he can to keep her around. Love reignites between them and they finally plan to remarry. At the end a telephone call about a hot news story on the route to their honeymoon location suggests that once again work will take over and romance will die.

A Life Less Ordinary

By the early sixties, the winds of change were blowing hard and film-makers no longer wanted to make movies which ostensibly promoted socially conservative morals. The questioning of accepted norms which had been portrayed as mistaken paths in the earlier films was rapidly becoming part of the mainstream. So movies in the sixties and beyond were presenting all kinds of other lifestyles as legitimate – and not just for women. It was an era in which all the conventions of the past were re-examined, challenged, satirised and undermined. Writing about romantic comedy, Frank Krutnik recognises that the changes in the genre (as with all genres) are bound up with worldview issues, not simply changing vogues:

> Endlessly recirculating, remobilising and rearticulating a stock repertoire of narrative and representational stratagems, the genre tells the same old story of heterosexual coupling. Only it is never quite the same old story. To succeed, romantic comedies must do more than simply redress themselves in contemporary fashions: they must engage with the shifting priorities and possibilities of intimate culture and with the broader cultural, social and economic spheres that organise its forms and meanings.[35]

Once again, new developments in the genre came about as a result of the enormous changes in western culture in the 1960s and beyond.[36] Christians, particularly those in older generations, tend to think of the period leading up to the sixties as one characterised by Christian morality, and assume that it has all been downhill since then. This is partly right, but once again we need to remind ourselves that modernism was as big an influence as Christianity, if not more so. The morality of that period was shaped by the modernist emphasis on rationality, order and control (and hence male domination) as well as by Christian faith. The fact that modernism had been allowed to become so intertwined with Christianity is part of the reason why, when people turned their back on the old to embrace the new, they rejected Christian faith as much as a modernist worldview.[37]

In the context of the film romance, the impact of the sexual liberation of the 1960s can hardly be over-estimated. Monogamy was disdained by a significant element of the younger generation (it is hard to imagine *Brief Encounter* being made in this period), and homosexuality began to be more publicly acceptable.[38] The attention of film, television and other media was caught by the most radical changes, and they brought them to a much wider audience. This of course has a normalising effect: putting this kind of lifestyle on screen, and presenting it as fun, dynamic and carefree suggests to those who are not part of the scene that they are missing out on the cool new lifestyle. Over subsequent decades, the values espoused by the counterculture have gradually become mainstream.

Love on the Rocks

Ironically, now that we find ourselves in a cultural situation in which, for many people, there are few limits, if any, on how to express one's sexuality, we seem to be more cynical about romance. As Nick Pollard notes, people have become disillusioned by love – perhaps because they have been hurt in the past, or because they have come to believe that love which lasts is a mere chimera: 'for many people, real love remains at best elusive, and at worst impossible.'[39] The term romance, 'has come to be almost a synonym for illusion'.[40]

And yet, cynical as our culture may be, it still cannot let go of love. *Closer* (Mike Nichols, 2004) and *Match Point* (Woody Allen, 2005) are at the cynical end, portraying relationships built on – and destroyed by – obsession, temptation and unbridled desire. At the other end of the spectrum, when Anna Scott (Julia Roberts) in *Notting Hill* (Roger Michell, 1999) tells William (Hugh Grant), 'I'm just a girl, standing in front of a boy, asking him to love her,' there are many who reach for a bucket[41] – but for many others it is genuinely moving. Brian (James McAvoy) in *Starter for Ten* (Tom Vaughan, 2006) struggles to negotiate his relationships with women, but ultimately he realises that real love is about something far deeper than looks. Postmodern fairy tales *Shrek* (Andrew Adamson and Vicky Jenson, 2001) and *Shrek 2* (Andrew Adamson, Kelly Asbury and Conrad Vernon, 2004) may be knowing parodies of all kinds of things, but ultimately they, too, affirm that love is about something much deeper than film-star beauty.

Responding to Genres

Genres may be difficult to pin down precisely, but they do seem to be a key part of how we engage with films. And, as the Western and romance show, their development is closely tied to shifts within the prevailing worldviews. We need, therefore, to be on the lookout for ways in which films reinforce the conventions of the genre – especially when those conventions result in a particular worldview being associated with the genre. And we need to be on the lookout for ways in which films go against the conventions, and in so doing express a subtly or radically different worldview.

When a number of films in a genre have challenged the conventions in similar ways, we might conclude that the genre is mutating once more. If so, we need to ask whether these departures from the traditions of the genre are becoming new conventions, and whether the genre as a whole is becoming associated with a different worldview. Those are not the kinds of questions we can answer quickly, but only after reflecting carefully on a significant number of films, alert to the connections and differences between them, and constantly asking what the various elements of the film reveal about worldviews.

Notes

1 Arroyo is specifically referring to *Mission Impossible*, but his point applies to many blockbuster movies. The quotation is from 'Mission: Sublime' in José Arroyo (ed.), *Action/Spectacle Cinema* (London: BFI, 2000) p. 23.

2 Thomas Shatz describes the development of genres as a move 'from straightforward storytelling to self-conscious formalism' in Leo Braudy and Marshall Cohen (eds.), *Film Theory and Criticism*, sixth edition (New York: Oxford University Press, 2004) p. 659.

3 Braudy and Cohen, *Film Theory and Criticism*, p. 658.

4 David Bordwell and Kristin Thompson, *Film Art: An Introduction*, sixth edition (New York: McGraw-Hill, 2001) p. 97.

5 For most of us there are film genres with which we are unfamiliar. Some are close enough to genres we are used to

for us to feel reasonably comfortable with them – German *Heimatfilme* (especially popular in the 1950s), centred on traditional small-town life and the triumph of love over social and economic barriers, for example. Others, like 'Bollywood' musicals based on classic Indian myths, can feel decidedly strange to many western filmgoers. Audiences want films within a particular genre to feel familiar, but at the same time, they expect them to be fresh and innovative rather than simply working through set formulae. The great directors will always bring something new to a genre even as they largely work within its established framework. I referred to auteur theory in Chapter 4. The idea, first developed by French theorists (notably François Truffaut) and popularised in English by Andrew Sarris, was to some extent a reaction against the idea of genres. For the auteur theorists, a director (usually) left a recognisable stamp on the work, and thereby transcended the limitations of the genre. Blending two genres can be a way of film-makers introducing some novelty while still essentially remaining within the traditions of one or both of the genres. *Bride and Prejudice* (Gurinder Chadha, 2004) is an entertaining example of this, combining the romance of Jane Austen's *Pride and Prejudice* with a westernised version of Bollywood traditions. It has helped to open up the pleasures of Indian musicals to a wider audience, at least in Britain.

6 For more on the supernatural within films and other media, see Tony Watkins (ed.), *Spooked: Talking About the Supernatural* (Milton Keynes: Damaris, 2006).

7 Bordwell and Thompson, *Film Art*, p. 99.

8 Indeed, Geoff Andrew argues that the famous stylised dance sequences of Busby Berkeley were coded erotic fantasies, referring to them as, 'impossibly dreamlike, lascivious worlds of luminous nubile flesh, ripe with visual (and often, through the songs, verbal) innuendo' (Geoff Andrew, *Directors A–Z: A Concise Guide to the Art of 250 Great Film-Makers* (London: Prion, 1999) p. 15.

9 The first Western was Edwin S. Porter's *The Great Train Robbery* in 1903, though it was shot on the east coast.

10 Edward Buscombe, *Cinema Today* (London: Phaidon, 2003) p. 133. The figures certainly bear this out: by 1910, around 20% of all Hollywood films were Westerns (Geoffrey Macnab, *Key Moments in Cinema: The History of Film and Film-makers* (London: Hamlyn, 2001) p. 93), rising to around a third in the 1950s (Mark Cousins, *The Story of Film* (London: Pavilion, 2004) p. 286).

11 Ford used Monument Valley as a location in ten of his films, and made ten Westerns (plus fifteen non-Westerns) with John Wayne. A number of those films are classic examples of the genre, as well as being some of Wayne's best films, including *Fort Apache* (1948), *She Wore a Yellow Ribbon* (1949), *Rio Grande* (1950), *The Searchers* (1956) and *How the West Was Won* (1962).

12 Jane Tompkins writes, 'Westerns invariably depict the same man – a man in flight from the domestic constraints of Victorian culture, afraid of losing mastery, at the centre of an endlessly repeated drama of death, inarticulateness, emotional numbness in a genre whose pattern of violence never varies.' (Jane Tompkins, *West of Everything: The Inner Life of Westerns* (Oxford: Oxford University Press, 1992) p. 39, quoted in Peter Francis, 'Clint Eastwood Westerns: Promised Land and Real Men' in Eric S. Christianson; Peter Francis and William R. Telford (eds.), *Cinéma Divinité: Religion, Theology and the Bible in Film* (London: SCM Press, 2005) p. 187.

13 James Monaco, *How to Read a Film: Movies, Media, Multimedia*, third edition (New York and Oxford: Oxford University Press, 2000) pp. 299–300.

14 Buscombe, *Cinema Today*, p. 133.

15 Cousins, *The Story of Film*, p. 287.

16 David Bordwell, *The Way Hollywood Tells It: Story and Style in Modern Movies* (Berkeley and Los Angeles: University of California Press, 2006).

17 Quoted in Macnab, *Key Moments in Cinema*, p. 96.

18 Glenn Erickson, 'Savant Review: The Man With No Name Trilogy', *DVDTalk.com*, 4 November 1999 – www.dvdtalk. com/dvdsavant/s90leonerev.html.

19 This title is in fact an invention of MGM's publicists in order to tie the three films together. Eastwood's character is referred to as Joe in *A Fistful of Dollars*, Monco in *For a Few Dollars More* and Blondie in *The Good, the Bad and the Ugly*. It is worth noting that Leone only hired Eastwood because he was cheap: Eastwood was keen to get into films, but Hollywood tended to spurn TV actors.

20 Stephen Prince, 'Genre and Violence in the Work of Kurosawa and Peckinpah' in Yvonne Tasker (ed.) *Action and Adventure Cinema* (Abingdon: Routledge, 2004) p. 331.

21 If you are interested in technical things, it was shot using Panavision anamorphic widescreen which makes use of a special camera lens to stretch the image vertically and make full use of the 35 mm film frame (otherwise a widescreen image shot onto standard 35 mm film stock wastes large areas of film at the top and bottom of the frame). When the film is projected, another special lens corrects the distortion resulting in a widescreen image. Leone's films were shot using Techniscope which only advanced the film half as far between each frame, thus fitting two unstretched widescreen frames in the same space on the film as a single conventional frame, though the quality is not as good.

22 For a detailed discussion, see Stephen Prince, 'The Aesthetic of Slow-Motion Violence in the Films of Sam Peckinpah' in Stephen Prince (ed.), *Screening Violence* (New Brunswick, New Jersey: Rutgers University Press, 2000) pp. 175–201. Prince makes a telling point when commenting on the shoot-outs which open and close the film: 'Through their dynamic energies, these montages convey the excitement and thrill of a film-maker no longer in moral control of his material to the viewer, who reacts accordingly. . . . [Peckinpah and Scorsese] could not disengage themselves, as artists, from the sensuous gratifications of assembling spectacularized violence. While

one should not doubt the sincerity of their belief in their own stated intentions, one may still be amazed at their blindness to their own artistic complicity in stimulating the aggressive reactions of their viewers.' (p. 198).

23 Peckinpah had already begun to explore this in *Ride the High Country* (1962) but it comes to its fullest expression in *The Wild Bunch*.

24 *The Wild Bunch* on IMDbPro.com – pro.imdb.com/title/tt0065214/taglines.

25 Bordwell describes this as 'almost blasphemous' in *The Way Hollywood Tells It*, p. 23.

26 For a detailed discussion of Eastwood's Westerns and what he communicates through them, see Peter Francis, 'Clint Eastwood Westerns: Promised Land and Real Men' in Eric S. Christianson; Peter Francis and William R. Telford (eds.), *Cinéma Divinité: Religion, Theology and the Bible in Film* (London: SCM Press, 2005) p. 187.

27 Quoted in Martin Scorsese and Michael Henry Wilson, *A Personal Journey with Martin Scorsese Through American Movies* (London: Faber and Faber, 1997) p. 43.

28 Arguably those characteristics are Christian values, but as we saw in Chapter 3, movies were influenced by Christianity as well as by modernism.

29 Peter Fraser and Vernon Edwin Neal, *ReViewing the Movies: A Christian Response to Contemporary Film* (Wheaton, Ill.: Crossway, 2000) p. 89.

30 David Bordwell, 'Story Causality and Motivation' in David Bordwell, Janet Staiger and Kristin Thompson, *The Classical Hollywood Cinema: Film Style and Mode of Production to 1960* (London: Routledge, 1988) p. 16. In *The Way Hollywood Tells It*, Bordwell argues that the romantic line of action is almost as prominent in most mainstream films since 1960.

31 Fraser and Neal, *ReViewing the Movies*, p. 90.

32 Jeanine Basinger, *A Woman's View: How Hollywood Spoke to Women, 1930–1960* (Hanover, NH.: Wesleyan University Press, 1993) p. 4.

33 Basinger, *A Woman's View*, p. 6–7.

34 David R. Shumway, 'Screwball Comedies: Constructing Romance, Mystifying Marriage' in Barry Keith Grant (ed.), *Film Genre Reader II* (Austin, Tex.: University of Texas Press, 1995) p. 385.

35 Frank Krutnik, 'Love Lies: Romantic Fabrication in Contemporary Romantic Comedy' in Peter William Evans and Celestino Deleyto, *Term of Endearment: Hollywood Romantic Comedy of the 1980s and 1990s* (Edinburgh: Edinburgh University Press, 1998) pp. 15–16.

36 This is, of course, why Bordwell, Staiger and Thompson's analysis of 'classical Hollywood cinema' only surveys films up until 1960. It is, however, fascinating that Bordwell's later book, *The Way Hollywood Tells It*, shows that despite enormous changes in content since 1960, the *way* Hollywood puts stories together still remains essentially the same.

37 An issue still facing the church is how to disentangle the modernist influence on Christianity in the west so that we can discern what is authentically biblical – and must therefore be held on to – and what is cultural (arising out of the general, modernist, plausibility structures), and is therefore open to renegotiation in our postmodern context.

38 We should bear in mind, however, that these starkly obvious aspects of the swinging sixties were not as widespread as we sometimes imagine. Away from the hip scenes in major population centres, many younger people continued to largely share the worldview and values of their parents.

39 Nick Pollard, 'Happily Never After?' in Tony Watkins (ed.), *Sex and the Cynics: Talking About the Search for Love* (Milton Keynes: Damaris, 2005) p. 1.

40 David Shumway, 'Screwball Comedies', p. 381.

41 It was voted the sixth most cheesy movie line in a survey of 2,000 filmgoers in 2004 ('Poll reveals cheesiest film lines', BBC News, 5 December 2004 – news.bbc.co.uk/1/hi/entertainment/film/4070771.stm).

Third Reel:
Responding to What Films
are Really Saying

7. What's it All About, Alfie?

Film and Our Deepest Longings

What are we all looking for in life? Happiness? Freedom? Love? Fulfilment? One of the reasons movies resonate strongly with us is because they show us characters who want the same things as us. More than anything Elinor and Marriane Dashwood (Emma Thompson and Kate Winslet in Ang Lee's 1995 adaptation of *Sense and Sensibility*) want to be loved. *Bend it Like Beckham* (Gurinder Chadha, 2002) shows the desperation of a teenage Sikh girl, Jesminder (Parminder Nagra), who wants to be free from family constraints so she can do what she most loves: play football. Miles (Paul Giamatti) and Jack (Thomas Haden Church), in *Sideways* (Alexander Payne, 2004), want little more than self-indulgence, with a week-long trip of wine tasting, golf and casual sex before Jack gets married. Mr Incredible (Craig T. Nelson) wants to feel fulfilled again, and to regain the sense of purpose he had when he worked as a superhero (*The Incredibles*, Brad Bird, 2004). In Hugh Hudson's 1981 classic *Chariots of Fire*, Harold Abrahams (Ben Cross) wants to win. So does Eric Liddell (Ian Charleson), but more than that, he wants to be faithful to God.

We connect with characters that we feel are like us, or whose goals are similar to ours. The more connection with the characters we feel, the more (usually) we love the film. Filmgoers naturally expect all kinds of other benefits from their visit to the cinema. Although some filmgoers want little more than to be kept entertained for a couple of hours, most want something more substantial – at least some of the time. We want to leave the cinema having been moved in some way or made to think; we want a sense of connection. Even those who only care about the surface level of a movie sometimes find that they unexpectedly connect with it and come out asking questions, privately if not openly with their friends. *The Matrix* had this effect on many people. In my experience, people can often be prompted to think about a film for the first time through a conversation in which someone asks some judicious questions. We will return to the question of how we respond, and help others respond, to movies in Chapter Eight. In this chapter I want to look at some of the connections we make with films – how they address the things that we most want in life. We make connections because films explore some of humanity's deepest desires. I will focus on a few which I believe are most fundamental, though it is important to realise that they overlap enormously.

Cry Freedom

Freedom may not seem to be an obvious concern, since most of us living in the west are not captives, and yet it is a fundamental human need. Psychologist Abraham Maslow identified five levels of human needs in his famous 'hierarchy of needs',[1] starting with the most basic physiological needs of air, water, nutrition, sleep, shelter and so on. We cannot even begin to think about freedom if these fundamental physiological needs are not met, as was illustrated in *Cast Away* (Robert Zemeckis, 2000). When schedule-obsessed FedEx manager Chuck Noland (Tom Hanks) washes up lost and alone on a desert island after a plane crash, his first thoughts are about finding fellow survivors and being rescued. But once he begins to become acutely aware of his need for the basics of food, water and shelter, he can think of nothing else – he is enslaved by these needs. Only when he has provided the bare necessities of life can he indulge in the 'luxury' of attracting the attention of rescue planes or thinking about escaping from the island.

Chuck is now operating at Maslow's second level: safety needs. We need to be secure, protected and stable. Maslow says that at this level we have a need for 'freedom from fear, from anxiety and chaos'.[2] It is clear that many within our supposedly free societies are not free in these ways. People live in fear of crime or terrorism (whether this fear is rational or not is beside the point); members of some communities even live in fear of moral anarchy. There are people who live in fear of physical or verbal abuse within their own homes. Many people are anxious about their finances, job security and a host of other issues. They long to be free from these fears. There is plenty of scope for dramatic tension with these issues in movies.

The horror genre is, arguably, a way of giving expression to, and confronting, primal human fears. Films like Robin Hardy's original 1973 version of *The Wicker Man* deal with our fear of the supernatural unknown; *The Others* (Alejandro Amenábar, 2001) is one of hundreds that explore our fear of death and what happens beyond.

Monster House (Gil Kenan, 2006), an animated comic horror for kids, is about children's fear of ill-tempered elderly neighbours and their spooky houses. Every exploration of fear reflects the basic desire to be free from that fear.

We can also crave freedom at Maslow's higher levels of human need. His third level is that of 'belongingness and love needs'.[3] Once Chuck Noland is able to survive, having met his requirements for food and safety, he begins to feel his loneliness acutely. His response is to treat a volleyball, which he calls Wilson, as his companion. If we are created as relational beings, then it seems to me that we cannot truly be free if that aspect of our nature cannot express itself. Like Chuck, we are effectively imprisoned in our loneliness. When Julie (Juliet Binoche) loses her husband and daughter in a car crash in *Three Colours: Blue* (Krzysztof Kieslowski, 1993), she tries to cut herself off from the past and start a new life alone. But she becomes locked into her grief, unable to begin to build a new life because she cannot deal emotionally with the pain caused by memories of the past. Eventually, the world and the needs of others force themselves onto Julie, and she is at last free to develop a new relationship and to throw herself into completing her husband's unfinished musical masterpiece.[4]

The fourth of Maslow's levels is esteem needs: the need for competence, confidence and self-respect on the one hand, and on the other hand, for the recognition, appreciation and respect of others. It is a problem faced by many of Woody Allen's protagonists, especially those he plays himself. In *Annie Hall* (1977) he is neurotic and obsessed with death; in *Hannah and Her Sisters* (1986) he is a neurotic hypochondriac; in *Crimes and Misdemeanors* (1989) he is unhappily married (and neurotic). There is always the sense that Allen, expressing himself through his characters, is desperate to be free from the hang-ups and neuroses which constrain his life. Longing for self-respect is a key motivating factor in a number of films – Rocky Balboa's need to go the distance in a fight for the world heavyweight boxing title in *Rocky* (John G. Avildsen, 1976), for example.

Maslow's top level is about personal fulfilment; he calls it self-actualization.[5] Again, there is an important connection with freedom. We may, reasons Maslow, have met all of our lower-level needs – we are well-fed, secure, loved, confident in ourselves and esteemed by others – yet still not be free to express our true inner selves. In *American Beauty* (Sam Mendes, 1999), Lester Burnham (Kevin Spacey) has an apparently perfect life, yet is deeply unfulfilled in his marriage and work. Robert Johnston points out that the roses grown by Lester's wife Caroline (Annette Bening) – the variety called American Beauty – are scentless: they look fantastic but have no substance.[6] Lester feels trapped in his life, likening himself at one point to a prisoner. One day he quits his job as an advertising executive and recalls his carefree days as a teenager with no responsibilities: 'All I did was party and get laid. I had my whole life ahead of me.' He decides to recapture the happiness of those days, so he buys the car he has always wanted, starts working out, takes drugs and fantasises about his daughter's beautiful best friend Angela (Mena Suvari). He is striving to be a teenager again, but what he really wants is to discover – and be true to – his real self. At one point he reflects, 'I feel like I've been in a coma for the past twenty years. And I'm just now waking up.' Ironically, almost as soon as Lester does wake up to who he really is and what is most important to him, he is killed. His reflections from beyond the grave open and close the film, and they are characterised by a sense of deep contentment since now he feels truly free.

Happy Ever After

All except the most pessimistic of people would rather be happy than not – but what we think we need in order to be happy varies enormously. The first four finders of golden tickets in *Charlie and the Chocolate Factory* (Tim Burton, 2005[7]) are obsessed with finding happiness in different ways: through food (Augustus Gloop), possessing everything (Veruca Salt), winning (Violet Beauregard) and entertainment (Mike Teavee). These children may be flat caricatures – in sharp contrast to protagonist Charlie Bucket (Freddie Highmore) – but adults can be nearly as single-minded in their pursuit of happiness. In *Catch Me If You Can* (Steven Spielberg, 2002) young Frank Abagnale Jr. (Leonardo DiCaprio) leaves home when his father has problems with his taxes and his mother has an affair. Believing that image is everything, he embarks on life as a conman. Masquerading as a Pan-Am co-pilot, he finances his hedonist lifestyle by cashing false cheques and submitting false expense claims. He buys smart suits and an Aston Martin, travels the world for free and sleeps with a succession of air stewardesses – all so that he can rediscover happiness.

In Her Shoes (Curtis Hanson, 2005) is the story of Maggie Feller (Cameron Diaz) who initially equates happiness with fun. She has plenty of entertainment in her party-filled life, but causes plenty of headaches for her sister Rose (Toni Collette). When Maggie ends up sleeping with Rose's fiancé, she escapes down to Florida to seek out their estranged grandmother Ella (Shirley MacLaine) who lives in a retirement complex. Maggie at first simply sponges off Ella and lazes around. But the old lady encourages her to take some responsibility and when Maggie's experienced eye for fashion comes to the rescue of one of Ella's friends, she develops a thriving business as a personal shopper. She finally comes to understand real happiness: not endless partying with no thought to the consequences of actions, but helping others to be happy. She is discovering happiness through personal fulfilment – a desire I will briefly consider in its own right shortly.

There are also, of course, protagonists who have more realistic and modest hopes for happiness than the hedonistic pursuit of wealth and entertainment. Happiness can come through family or friends or simply positively embracing one's lot in life, as for Viktor Navorski (Tom Hanks) who is stranded in an airport terminal for months in *The Terminal* (Steven Spielberg, 2004). For Jewish Italian Guido (Roberto Benigni) in the Academy Award-winning film about the holocaust which he directed, *Life is Beautiful* (1997), happiness is about having the right attitude. He is relentlessly cheerful as he sees all of life as one big fairy tale. Even when he and his wife and son are taken to a Nazi concentration camp, he is determined to help his son Giosuè be happy by making him believe that they are part of a big game. He tells him that the guards are cruel because they want to win the prize, a tank. Even in such circumstances, it seems some degree of happiness is possible because it ultimately comes from within, not from our circumstances.

A film which looks at the question of happiness more explicitly than most, with strong echoes of Ecclesiastes, is *Thirteen Conversations About One Thing* (Jill Sprecher,

2001). It is about multiple protagonists with momentarily intersecting plot lines. They are all preoccupied with happiness: what it is, and whether it can ever be found. Walker (John Turturro) seems to have changed after being the victim of a mugging. He tells his wife Patricia (Amy Irving) that he wants, 'What everyone wants: to experience life; to wake up enthused; to be happy,' but soon he despairs of the possibility of happiness. Hotshot attorney Troy (Matthew McConaughey) celebrates a court triumph in a bar, apparently experiencing unbridled happiness. But when a stranger Gene (Alan Arkin) suggests that it is just luck, Troy insists, 'Luck is the lazy man's excuse.' Troy sees happiness as something to be worked for – but later it evaporates in an instant when he knocks down a young woman and drives away. At work Gene is intensely irritated by a perpetually happy colleague Wade (William Wise) who sees happiness as a state of mind: accepting whatever life brings and always seeing the good in it. At the end of the film, bandages around Patricia's wrists suggest her intense misery. But Gene, with whom she has no connection, happens to be in the same train carriage. He has come to understand how actions impact on others. As he alights to wait for his connection, he gives Patricia a brief, tentative wave, bringing the first smile to Patricia's face.

Love Actually

Love, as we saw in the previous chapter, has always been a central concern in films – and not just those from Hollywood. It is a far deeper concern in many films, however, than simply having a romantic line of action alongside a work-related one. Rather than merely heading for some neat resolution after a number of setbacks and difficulties, they explore the nature of love and its centrality to human nature. The publicity tagline of *Moulin Rouge!* (Baz Lurhmann, 2001) makes clear just how vital love is: 'The greatest thing you'll ever learn is just to love and be loved in return.' On the other hand, films can spout complete nonsense, such as the famous line, 'Love means never having to say you're sorry,' in *Love Story* (Arthur Hiller, 1970). Judy (Barbra Streisand) quotes this line in *What's Up, Doc?* (Peter Bogdanovich, 1972), but Howard (Ryan O'Neal, who had starred in *Love Story)* retorts, 'That's the dumbest thing I've ever heard.'

One of the most praised of all romantic comedies is Rob Reiner's *When Harry Met Sally* (1989, scripted by Nora Ephron who went on to both write and direct *Sleepless in Seattle* (1993) and *You've Got Mail* (1998)). It charts a couple's friendship from the time they first meet through various encounters over the course of the next twelve years. During this time they both fail to find love with others, but their friendship grows stronger. Harry (Billy Crystal) denies that it is possible for a man and woman to be friends without sex being a factor. Eventually, Harry turns up declaring that he loves every last little idiosyncrasy of the woman (Meg Ryan) who has become his dearest friend, the person that he most wants to talk to before he goes to sleep at night, the woman that he wants to spend the rest of his life with. We viewers, of course, know that these two are made for each other from the outset (quite literally, since they are fictional creations) so we are frustrated at the reversals along the way, and we almost see Harry's and Sally's other relationships as infidelities. The way their love grows out of long friendship is in contrast to many love-at-first-sight relationships in films, or at least relationships which are primarily sexual from the outset.

Love is so elemental, though, that it can become all-consuming, driving those obsessed by it to do terrible things. The most obvious of these actions is infidelity, featured in countless movies over the years. Some films do not even seem to consider the ethical side of this, presenting affairs as normal or even as something very positive. *Out of Africa* (Sydney Pollack, 1985), *The Piano* (Jane Campion, 1993) and *The Bridges of Madison County* (Clint Eastwood, 1995) are just three examples of this tendency. Other films, however, do explore some of the consequences and implications. The sense of betrayal is an important element in *Sliding Doors* (Peter Howitt, 1998), for example. Deception and guilt are almost inevitable consequences of an affair – explored power-fully in *Separate Lies* (Julian Fellowes, 2005) among many others. In Woody Allen's *Match Point* (2005) they even drive Chris (Jonathan Rhys-Meyers) to murder his lover Nola (Scarlett Johansson). Violence and murder (or attempted murder) are more normally associated with the wronged party getting revenge – whether the betrayed spouse, as in *Dial M for Murder* (Alfred Hitchcock, 1954)[8], or a jilted lover, as in *Fatal Attraction* (Adrian Lyne, 1987).

Some of the saddest stories played out on the silver screen are the romantic tragedies. Film-makers know that there is enormous pathos in the death, betrayal or abandonment of a lover. In presenting us with such heart-rending stories, we are reinforced in our feeling that love is supremely important. If we do not have it, we should find it; if we do have it, we should do all in our power to hang on to it, or to make the most of it while we can. *The Remains of the Day* (James Ivory, 1993) is intensely sad because butler Stevens (Anthony Hopkins) and housekeeper Miss Kenton (Emma Thompson) are so repressed by their pre-war culture that they are unable to express their love for each other. We feel that this is what they need, yet they – Stevens in particular – deny it to themselves. When I first watched *New York, New York* (Martin Scorsese, 1977), the inability of Jimmy Doyle (Robert De Niro) and Francine Evans (Liza Minnelli) to put their love before their careers made me miserable for days afterwards.

The Secret of My Success

Fulfilment clearly overlaps with freedom, happiness and love. I have already noted when discussing *In Her Shoes* that Maggie Feller wants happiness, but does not care about personal fulfilment. When she finally discovers, almost by accident, that real happiness comes through being fulfilled, she seems to be functioning at Maslow's fifth level and is experiencing some 'self-actualization'. Many movies show us people who know already that happiness is ultimately about finding fulfilment, and who recognise that fulfilment is somehow deeper because it is about being true to our nature and personality.

In *Gattaca* (Andrew Niccol, 1997), for example, Vincent (Ethan Hawke) dreams of being a navigator on space missions. But he was born without the assistance of the local geneticist, unlike most of his contemporaries, putting him at a distinct disadvantage. His DNA was not selected for intelligence, strength, stamina or whatever, and he struggles with imperfect eyesight and the statistical possibility that he may develop a fatal heart condition. There is no way he can fulfil his dream – except by dropping out of mainstream society and becoming 'invalid', buying a new genetic identity on the black market, and training hard to be as physically fit and mentally sharp as any of his genetically-advantaged rivals for places at Gattaca Space Academy. He succeeds in achieving his dream – a triumph of human will over circumstances – but it is never seen in terms of mere happiness. Achieving one's potential is a crucial aspect. Films about artificial intelligence often explore this in interesting ways. David (Haley Joel Osment) in *A.I. Artificial Intelligence* (Steven Spielberg, 2001) and Sonny (the robot) in *I, Robot* (Alex Proyas, 2004) both develop what are assumed to be uniquely human characteristics – in particular the ability to dream – and are able to experience some sense of personal fulfilment.

Fulfilment can be achieved through some kind of spiritual or mystical experience – as in *Field of Dreams* (Phil Alden Robinson, 1989), *Kundun* (Martin Scorsese, 1997) and *Star Wars* (George Lucas, 1977) – or by 'creating ourselves through personal choice or commitment'[9] as in *Forrest Gump* (Robert Zemeckis, 1994). Fulfilment can be achieved through doing good to others, as in *Pay it Forward* (Mimi Leder, 2001) and *Amélie* (Jean-Pierre Jeunet, 2001). In *Kramer vs. Kramer* (Robert Benton, 1979), Ted Kramer (Dustin Hoffman) finally achieves real fulfilment in life through his role as a father. When his wife Joanna (Meryl Streep) leaves him and son Billy in order to 'find herself', Ted is landed with childcare duties as well as the career that has so far consumed all his energies. Eventually, however, raising Billy becomes more important to him than anything.

In the beginning of the film you have a negative
father who works until late, swaps sexist jokes with
his boss, and comes home to find that his wife is
leaving him. He is not very good for the first few
days, but fatherhood changes him and he becomes
perfect.[10]

Million Dollar Baby (Clint Eastwood, 2004) sees the loss of
fulfilment as the worst kind of tragedy. At the start of the
film, Maggie (Hilary Swank) is desperate to box but, in
the opinion of Frankie (Eastwood), she is starting too late
in life. Besides which, he doesn't train girls. Through her
determination she wins Frankie over and discovers some
real skill. Frankie becomes her trainer and she eventually
gets to fight for the world championship: her greatest
dream come true. But disaster strikes and Maggie is
paralysed from the neck down. Unable to do anything for
herself, she considers herself to be in a worse position
than if she was dead. She can no longer do the one thing
she loves and pleads with Frankie to kill her.

Protagonists frequently discover fulfilment after
pursuing the wrong goals. The character development
that comes as a result of difficulties faced by protagonists
enables them to discover what really matters in life. It is
then associated with a process of moral reform as a
character's arc takes them on a journey from corruption
to integrity, from weakness to strength, from treachery to
loyalty or from cowardice to courage. When Phil
Connors (Bill Murray) discovers that he is somehow
reliving the same day over and over again in *Groundhog
Day* (Harold Ramis, 1993), he soon realises that he has the
opportunity to enjoy himself with no consequences. He
throws himself into the pursuit of happiness, robbing
banks and seducing women. He also attempts to seduce

Rita (Andie MacDowell), but fails day after day. Soon his hedonism turns to despair and he commits suicide, but still he wakes up again on the same day. Eventually, he directs his attention to becoming a better person. He learns French and becomes a skilled pianist and an expert ice sculptor. He also starts to lose his cynicism, self-centredness and arrogance. He discovers real pleasure in helping people and improving their lives. And as he becomes focused on the concerns of others, he becomes a kind and delightful person. It is deeply fulfilling in itself. Having reached that point, he wins Rita's love without even trying because he is at last able to genuinely love.

A Peace of the Action

Happiness, freedom, love and fulfilment are all profoundly important, but I believe that there is something even more fundamental to which they point. Think back to Genesis 1–3, and the creation of human beings in the image and likeness of God. As I noted in Chapter 1, this means that we are relational beings, created to be in relationship with God and with each other (most intimately in the spiritual and physical union of marriage). The picture which Genesis gives us is one of peace between humanity and God, between one human and another, and between human beings and their environment. We infer that Adam and Eve were at peace with themselves too. They were at home physically, emotionally and spiritually. This is the biblical understanding of *shalom* (peace) – an all-embracing state of well-being. Shalom arises out of peace with God, and it was wrecked by the Fall. No longer was there harmony with the environment or peace between human beings;

no longer was there peace with God or within each human heart. Adam and Eve were expelled from their physical home (3:22–24) with no possibility of return. The rest of the Bible is the unfolding story of restoring humanity to its home.[11] Amazingly, the Gospels tell the story of God making his home with us in the person of his son Jesus Christ, but being expelled from our world at the crucifixion. Human rebellion could not keep him out, however, and having returned once in the resurrection, he will return again to bring final judgement and ultimate salvation. Finally, the great cry will go up in heaven: 'Look, the home of God is now among his people! He will live with them, and they will be his people. God himself will be with them.'[12] True peace – shalom – will finally, ultimately, be restored.

Meanwhile, though, we human beings are constantly trying to recover that peace for ourselves. We were made for peace with God, peace with each other and peace with ourselves, yet all of them are out of our reach in any ultimate sense. And so we chase after all sorts of things that we think will restore that peace to us. We pursue happiness because we mistake it for peace, and we imagine that wealth, possessions, power, status or health will give us the happiness we crave. Happiness is a pale reflection of peace and, as many people have discovered, it is possible to have everything you ever wanted and still lack peace. And you can give it all away again and still not find true peace, though you are possibly closer to it. We crave freedom because we imagine that our lack of peace is because we are constrained – perhaps not physically but socially, emotionally or morally. Freedom is part of peace, but it is not the entirety of it.

We strive to be fulfilled or self-actualized, assuming that everything else will be put into perspective once we are. But we can discover that the sense of fulfilment does not always last – not least because the fulfilment we often seek is only for this world. We are made to be fulfilled, but true fulfilment is tied to true peace, which is why Paul focused all his energies on reaching the end of the race.[13] More than almost anything, we long to love and be loved. This gets us much closer to the heart of true peace since, above all, peace is relational. Indeed, we find that relationships are the things that give us most happiness, that enable us to feel most free and that make us most fulfilled. But it only gets us part way there, since while it may give us peace with each other and ourselves, it still does not achieve peace with God which remains out of our grasp. As Eddie Jessup (William Hurt) says in *Altered States* (Ken Russell, 1980):

> We're all trying to fulfil ourselves, understand ourselves, get in touch with ourselves, face the reality of ourselves, explore ourselves, expand ourselves. Ever since we dispensed with God we've got nothing but ourselves to explain this meaningless horror of life.

Spirituality is the only route left – it is, of course, the one way that we actually can find true peace. But even this fails to bring shalom for many people since they assume that it is something they have to *do*, to *achieve*, instead of something to accept as a gift from God. We have within us a deep, instinctive urge to be lost in worship, but since many of us do not even recognise it, never mind understand how it should be expressed, we lose ourselves in other things instead. This is a deeply spiritual matter – even if whatever we attempt to lose ourselves in is not obviously spiritual at all. Our attempts to find happiness, freedom, love and fulfilment can all be second-best things in which we lose ourselves – expressing that instinctive urge to worship in the wrong ways. The first commandment – 'You shall have no other gods before me (Ex. 20:3) – provides the only way for this urge to be expressed safely, because, as Craig Gay says, 'When we lose sight of God, we also lose sight of ourselves.'[14] The result is that we become idolaters, worshipping – giving our lives to, sacrificing ourselves to – that which is not God. If God is not at the centre of our lives, everything we chase after is a substitute for God; everything we pursue in life is an attempt to find ultimate peace.

I would argue, therefore, that all narratives are at some level giving expression to this longing for peace. Some of them explicitly focus on peace, though not usually in the ultimate sense of shalom. In *The Constant Gardener* (Fernando Meirelles, 2005), when the wife (Rachel Weisz) of diplomat Justin Quayle (Ralph Fiennes) is killed in Kenya, Justin sets about discovering the reasons for her death. When he ultimately sacrifices himself in order to complete his wife's work by drawing attention to it, he welcomes his imminent death because he will, finally, be at peace. Playboy Alfie (Jude Law in Charles Shyer's 2004 version[15]) lives entirely for his own satisfaction, sleeping with any woman who takes his fancy while constantly oozing style and charm. After a series of setbacks, he surprises himself by falling in love with an older woman. But when he is dumped for a younger man, he realises how shallow his existence is. Finally he reflects:

Despite my best efforts I'm beginning to feel some small cracks in my faux finish . . . My life's my own, but I don't have peace of mind. And if you don't have that, you've got nothing.

Andrew Niccol's *Lord of War* (2005) is extremely powerful for the very reason that it is not ultimately redemptive. Arms dealer Yuri Orlov (Nicolas Cage) plies his particular trade because he is good at it and makes lots of money. He is such a strong central protagonist that we cannot help but identify with him to some extent. We want him to be redeemed in some way. He goes legitimate for a while at the urging of his wife – but is tempted back for one more job. Yuri is repeatedly faced with the immorality of his profession, and pays a high price for it when his brother is killed, he is arrested by the FBI, his parents disown him and his family abandon him. In spite of this, he does not conclude that he was wrong to return to gun-running. Instead, he throws himself back into it. After a film which has powerfully shown the horrific consequences of illegal arms, the fact that he coolly continues with it (followed by a closing title revealing that the biggest arms dealers in the world are the permanent members of the UN Security Council) reinforces our sense of moral outrage. Yuri is unchanged: there is no redemption for this man, nor has he wanted it. What he *has* wanted is to find peace which, ironically, he finds through peddling arms because that is what he is good at. At the end of the film he reflects, 'You know who's going to inherit the Earth? Arms dealers. Because everyone else is too busy killing each other. That's the secret to survival. Never go to war. Especially with yourself.'

Lord of War may be unredemptive, but it nevertheless shows the human longing for peace, for shalom – the deepest need of all. Many people in our society are unable to articulate this longing because they are entirely unaware of the biblical concept of peace. They feel this ache in their spirits – at least in their most reflective and honest moments, when they are not using entertainment and activity to mask it – and try to find a solution in things that, good as they may be, are not good enough. All we know and can focus on are the reflections and shadows of shalom. Freedom still leaves us enslaved since we are all slaves to sin; happiness is not enough because life is too fragile and unpredictable; love is not enough, because people will always disappoint us at some stage; even personal fulfilment fails to go far enough because it does not reconcile us with God himself. True freedom comes through knowing the truth,[16] but the truth is a person: Jesus himself.[17] Once we find true peace with God through his son, the way to true fulfilment, love, happiness and freedom is open. We will not experience all this fully before we reach our ultimate home,[18] the new heavens and the new earth, but we can experience them developing in new ways in our lives.

These issues of freedom, happiness, love, fulfilment and peace relate closely to the fifth worldview question from Chapter 2: What is the fundamental problem confronting all human beings, and what is the solution? Or, to put it a different way, what do we most need in life? As we engage thoughtfully with films, we will inevitably find ourselves reflecting on the film-makers' ideas about what makes a person complete. There are other possibilities besides the five which I have looked at in this chapter, of course, and we must recognise that they are not always being offered as ultimate solutions to the problems facing humanity as a whole, but rather as solutions to the needs of the individual protagonist. Nevertheless, underpinning them all is this deeply instinctive longing for shalom. We need to recognise how echoes of this yearning crop up in films, and to help others come to a fuller understanding of what the human heart needs above all.

Notes

1 See Abraham Maslow, *Motivation and Personality*, second edition (New York and London: Harper and Row, 1970) pp. 35–47.

2 Maslow, *Motivation and Personality*, p. 39.

3 Maslow, *Motivation and Personality*, p. 43.

4 *Blue* is a very deliberate exploration of freedom as it is the first part of Kieslowski's much-acclaimed *Three Colours* trilogy based around the French republican ideals of liberty, equality (*White*, 1994), and fraternity (*Red*, 1994).

5 Although the term was not coined by Abraham Maslow, it was he who popularised it. He wrote in 1943, 'What a man *can* be, he *must* be. This need we may call self-actualization' (*Psychol Rev* L 382). He repeats this in *Motivation and Personality*, p. 46, adding 'A man must be true to his own nature.'

6 Robert K. Johnston, *Useless Beauty: Ecclesiastes Through the Lens of Contemporary Film* (Grand Rapids, Mich.: Baker Academic, 2004) p. 58.

7 The same is obviously true of Mel Stuart's 1971 version of Roald Dahl's story, which he entitled *Willy Wonka & the Chocolate Factory*.

8 Remade as *A Perfect Murder* (Andrew Davis, 1998), the story is actually one of a thwarted intention to take revenge.

9 Brian Godawa, *Hollywood Worldviews: Watching Films with Wisdom and Discernment* (Downers Grove, Ill.: IVP, 2002) p. 53.

10 Stella Bruzzi, interviewed by Marco Zee-Jotti, 'Bringing Up Daddy', *Filmwaves*, Issue 30, Winter 2006, pp. 14–15. Bruzzi prefaces her comments about Ted Kramer by noting, 'There is a range of films that suggest that Hollywood does not like the single mother . . . On the whole mothers tend to be

positive when they are in a stable domestic situation.'

11 There are foreshadowings of it in the Old Testament, in particular as Israel entered the promised land of Canaan and during the reign of David, but there are also acute periods of homelessness (slavery in Egypt, the annihilation of the northern kingdom, the Babylonian exile) and times when Israel was full of violence and idolatry: Israel may have been at home physically but they were not at home with God.

12 Revelation 21:3 (NLT).

13 Philippians 3:12–14.

14 Craig Gay, *The Way of the (Modern) World or, Why It's Tempting to Live As if God Doesn't Exist* (Carlisle: Paternoster, 1998).

15 This remake of Lewis Gilbert's classic 1966 film starring Michael Caine (itself a version of Bill Naughton's original play) reflects a very different social context. Both films conclude with Alfie wondering about one of life's key questions: 'What's it all about?'

16 John 8:32.

17 John 14:6.

18 John 14:2 (NLT).

8. The Soul of Cinema

Responding to Films

The impact films have on us is not so much because of how much time we spend watching them, but, I believe, because of the way we encounter them. Film-watching is a deliberate exercise. We actively choose to go to the cinema and pay good money for the experience – hence the frustration over watching a complete dud is greater than if we watched it on television. We are also intentional when we decide which DVDs to buy or (to a lesser extent) rent – and increasingly when we decide what movies we will download from the Internet. Going to the local multiplex to watch a movie tends to be especially reflective in that our viewing is more active than when we are slouched on the sofa at home. Not only have we made a very deliberate choice about what to watch, but the darkened auditorium, big screen and high-volume surround-sound create a much more vivid experience. These factors combine to focus our attention in a quite intense way. We may be goggle-eyed and slack-jawed, but we are soaking up the experience and, as I noted in Chapter 1, we are very likely to talk about it with our friends afterwards.

With powerful experiences like this, it is no surprise that films do influence people at some level or other. In particular, they can contribute to changes in people's worldviews, usually gradually but occasionally dramatically. As I have noted previously, movies both reflect and shape culture. They reflect culture in that they show us something of the diversity of perspectives, beliefs and attitudes around us, and communicate the worldview of the film-makers. As we have seen, the film-makers may not be setting out to deliberately promote their own worldview, but it nevertheless undergirds everything they do. Nicholas Wolterstorff says that works of art 'are not simply the oozings of subconscious impulses; they are the result of beliefs and goals on the part of the artist.'[1] We as viewers will pick up much of the worldview which is being communicated – whether we realise it or not. The structure of the narrative, the use of genre conventions and the cinematic techniques encourage people (whether subtly or blatantly) to take on board some perspectives and to reject others. It is vital to realise that all of us, to some degree, are influenced by at least some of what we see – even if we believe ourselves to be impervious to its effects. So movies help to shape our culture, contributing over time to the strengthening or weakening of the plausibility structures which shape society so decisively. I think it is rare that an individual film has a radical impact on its own, but the effect is cumulative. We will return to this shortly, but first we need to note the implication of all this for the way we respond to a movie.

First, it is clear that we do need to make some response. We are failing in our responsibilities as Christians if we do not do so. If I am to love God with my mind and love my neighbour as myself,[2] I really must think carefully about the culture I am part of – the culture which is constantly both God-reflecting and God-resisting. Second, we need to respond personally to what we see, and we need to respond in relationship to others – both Christians and those who do not share our faith.

Responding Personally

The primary response to a film is inevitably personal. Any movie will impact on me in very particular ways because of the kind of person I am, the interests I have, the knowledge I have accumulated and the experiences I have had. Other people will not respond in the same way. A strong sense of connection with the film can make viewers more open to the ideas within it and more sympathetic to the values it portrays. Conversely, a lack of connection can make viewers feel very hostile to a film's ideas and values – and the lack of connection may be because of a worldview clash. A strong atheist is likely to have a deep-seated resistance to the worldview and perhaps even the story of *The Chronicles of Narnia: The Lion, the Witch and the Wardrobe* (Andrew Adamson, 2005), for example.

Since this book is about worldviews in films, much of what we have considered has been at the largely intellectual and moral levels of beliefs and values. But it is important to realise that our personal response to a movie must also take place at a number of levels, some of which impact us more strongly than others. Some viewers are caught up in the plot and need to work hard to notice the details of characterisation or *mise-en-scène*. Others, amazingly, do not even seem to care about plot. Two filmgoers interviewed in a study of audience responses to *Judge Dredd* (Danny Cannon, 1995) just wanted 'lots of blood', explosions, impressive effects and dead bodies. They were utterly dismissive of watching a film for its story: 'We don't watch it for that! We watch it for the action, well I do, anyway.'[3] For some people, the dialogue is what holds their attention – perhaps because they are generally very people-oriented. Others are very visual and respond most strongly to the aesthetic beauty of the cinematography. Christians can sometimes get completely caught up on the morality of a film. If we really want to engage well with films, it is important that we learn to respond to films at a variety of levels – including the aesthetic and emotional dimensions of the movie. We should neither be like some film theorists who have a solely academic approach to films, nor like those movie critics who only think about a film's entertainment value. Our engagement with any aspect of our culture should not be either entirely intellectual or entirely non-intellectual. Rather, as Christians who understand what it means to be God's image-bearers, we should respond holistically since film impacts us at different levels of our being. Let me summarise some of the levels at which we need to respond:

The aesthetic level

The aesthetic dimension is immensely important to life – more so, I am convinced, than we often allow for. Within the church (at least, within the Protestant tradition from which I come) we have sometimes seen it as an optional extra. It might not be stated quite so baldly, but there has at times been a tendency to take a rather functional approach to life. This is largely a result of the false division of life into the sacred and the secular. Creativity expressed within the 'sacred' dimension – church music, religious poetry, explicitly Christian art – is all well and good, but any form of art outside the sacred sphere is dismissed as secular. It is regarded at best as neutral; often as worldly and corrupting. This means that certain expressions of creativity and the appreciation of beauty have not always been given the place they deserve in our theology or in our worldview. Entire modes of creative expression have been written off at times in church history: dancing, popular music and cinema have been especially disparaged.

But the aesthetic dimension is an integral part of God's creation. Genesis 2:9 notes that trees were 'pleasing to the eye' as well as having their more functional role of providing food. Later in the chapter, when describing the location of Eden, our attention is drawn to the gold, aromatic resin and onyx present there (v. 12). It is significant that these three substances are valued for their beauty rather than for their usefulness.[4] Our human creativity is a reflection of God's creativity – whether it is used for supposedly sacred or secular purposes. John Calvin insisted that 'all truth is God's truth', but we could equally say that all beauty is God's beauty. Just as any genuine truth which we discover must be consistent with God and his nature, so, too, any beauty is either created by God, or is a product of God's image and likeness manifesting itself in the artist. The purpose to which beauty is put is another matter – a matter of truth, integrity and morality, but we can and must value that which is beautiful.

Our aesthetic appreciation works at a deep, instinctive, visceral level and we cannot always clearly articulate how something impacts on us. When Andy Dufresne (Tim Robbins) plays Mozart's 'Canzonetta sull'aria' from *The Marriage of Figaro* over the prison tannoy in *The*

Shawshank Redemption (Frank Darabont, 1994), our hearts soar with the music, and when Morgan Freeman's voice-over tells us that, 'at that moment every man in Shawshank [Prison] felt free,' we know exactly what he means.[5] When we see Jackie Elliot weeping with the emotion of seeing the ballet *Swan Lake* in *Billy Elliot* (Stephen Daldry, 2000), and then see Billy's extraordinarily majestic, graceful leap into the air when he makes his entrance as principal dancer, we, too weep with joy. This is what Billy (Jamie Bell) started working towards years before. He has triumphed over his social background and over prejudice, and that wonderful leap to Tchaikovsky's stirring music sums it all up. When we see the beauty of the Irish countryside in *The Wind that Shakes the Barley* (Ken Loach, 2006), we are stirred by its wild beauty and tranquillity, and it forms an important counterpoint to the violent events portrayed.

We feel these moments deep down inside; we are moved emotionally. These are transcendent experiences, not intellectual ones, and many non-religious people regard the experience of great beauty as a spiritual thing. This is why I have come to feel that the experience of beauty is somehow associated with the experience of hope. The beauty takes us beyond ourselves, pointing to something greater. Even Billy Elliot's dance of rage, to the soundtrack of The Jam's 'A Town Called Malice', shouts at us that there is more to life than his father realises, and makes us feel the injustice of stopping this boy from developing his exceptional gifts. Despite the fact that Billy ultimately crashes into a corrugated iron gate at the end of the road – an obvious metaphor for the constraints on Billy – we still feel that such talent must eventually triumph over the circumstances.

There is a wider sense to this aesthetic level of response,

though. Identifying the aesthetic dimension exclusively with superficial, obvious beauty is too narrow. It also includes order, coherence, diversity and rightness (something being right for its context – which can be related to the functional dimension), truth and other aspects which are not obviously 'beautiful'. Jeremy Begbie argues that a Christian understanding of beauty should be grounded in 'the transformation of the disorder of creation in the history of Jesus Christ'.[6] That is, a central aspect of redemption through Christ is the undoing of disorder resulting from the Fall – both within individual lives and within creation as a whole. *The Lake House* (Alejandro Agresti, 2006) is not a great film, but it does celebrate the architecture of Chicago and reminds us what extraordinarily wonderful things humans can do with their environments, even in cities. It reminds us that the best architecture needs to work sympathetically with the natural light, and connect with the natural surroundings. For many people, a glass and steel skyscraper is hardly beautiful, yet it can still be aesthetically satisfying. The scenes of the D-Day invasion in *Saving Private Ryan* (Steven Spielberg, 1998) were not beautiful, but they were aesthetically powerful. Responding aesthetically, then, is not simply about looking for moving examples of beauty within films, but includes recognising other aesthetic values. In particular, in the case of films, it includes the recognition of excellence in every aspect of the film-making and writing. *Fight Club* (David Fincher, 1999), for example, is harsh and disturbing but it is extremely cleverly written, powerfully acted and brilliantly directed.

The emotional level

Movies like Steven Spielberg's *Schindler's List* (1993) and

Munich (2005) have little *beauty* within them, but they are powerful stories and (for many viewers) excellent films. They are at times disturbing, even harrowing, depictions of traumatic moments from the last century, and their excellence as films arises in part from the honesty with which they handle the events within them.[7] Such powerful films cannot help but affect us emotionally and it is right that they do so; if we approach them dispassionately and clinically (in our concern to analyse worldviews, perhaps), then we do not allow the film to communicate with us as the director intended. One of the difficulties here is that some viewers regard the emotionally intense moments of such films as being manipulative. Spielberg in particular is frequently criticised for playing with the emotions of the audience, manufacturing a lump in the throat rather than seriously engaging with the issues. Others, though, see the creation of emotional experiences as a vital element of films. If Spielberg causes viewers to feel in a certain way, he is enabling us to feel like he does at that point. Whether or not we agree with him when we further reflect on the film is not the point: as a film-maker he has enabled us (legitimately) to identify with his perspective for a while.

Regardless of whether or not emotional manipulation is at work, we *ought* to come away from a viewing of *Schindler's List* or *Hotel Rwanda* (Terry George, 2004) overwhelmed with grief at the horror of man's inhumanity, and profoundly moved at the courage of people like Oskar Schindler (Liam Neeson) and Paul Rusesabagina (Don Cheadle) to do what they can in the face of it. We should weep with anguished joy at the irrepressibly enthusiastic way in which Guido (Roberto Benigni) makes concentration camp life bearable for his son, in *Life is Beautiful* (Benigni, 1997). We ought to feel the agony of the choice facing Justine (Jennifer Aniston) in *The Good Girl* (Manuel Arteta, 2002): to head off down the open road with her criminal lover Holden (Jake Gyllenhaal) for a life of freedom, passion and excitement, or to do the right thing, telling the truth and returning to her husband, despite the lovelessness of her marriage and the dullness of her small-town life. We should ache for Rick (Humphrey Bogart) as he overcomes his feelings for his former lover Ilsa (Ingrid Bergman) and helps her to escape the Nazi authorities with her resistance leader husband (Paul Henreid) in *Casablanca* (Michael Curtiz, 1942). Feeling the emotional power of a story is an important part of our engagement with it, and it may be that sometimes we have to watch a film once to feel its emotional force, and a second time to analyse its worldview.

The ethical level

Questions of ethics are deeply intertwined with questions of worldview as we have already seen in previous chapters. However, we do need to respond to a film at an explicitly ethical level as opposed to just understanding the ethical dimensions of its worldview. There are four interrelated aspects to this. The most important question to ask is whether or not the film is being truthful. That is, does it deal with the issues of life with integrity? Is the world reflected in the film authentic, in that it shows something of the glory of humanity created in God's image, or of the struggle and difficulty of life in a fallen world?[8] Gordon Matties writes that we should

> approach movies 'dialogically,' that is, by recognizing ways in which movies either illuminate our world and our lives with glimmers of transcendence or cast shadows of brokenness and alienation.[9]

Babette's Feast (Gabriel Axel, 1987) is both a wonderful celebration of the great gift of food and an indictment of faith that has fossilised into mere religious observance. Peter Fraser discusses the integrity with which *Brief Encounter* (David Lean, 1945) handles the subject of adultery:

> . . . the characters face a situation that is quite plausible, and they react to it quite plausibly. . . . That adultery is wrong and that we wished it would never happen and that we hope and pray that we never are tempted in that way is beside the point. The point is that is does happen, even to 'good' people . . . and they suffer as a result. . . . *Brief Encounter* begs us to feel compassion for human beings in a broken world who want to be happy, but do not have the strength on their own to accomplish that.[10]

In his book *Useless Beauty*,[11] Robert Johnston discusses a number of films which express the brokenness of the world as well as a 'fragile beauty'. One of his examples is *Monster's Ball* (Marc Forster, 2001), which focuses on two profoundly broken people. Hank is a prison officer (Billy Bob Thornton) who is in charge of the death row team. His harsh treatment of his son results in the young man's suicide. Leticia (Halle Berry) is the widow of the executed man. Her grief is compounded when her son is killed by a hit and run driver. Hank's humanity overcomes his racism to help her, and they gradually develop a relationship. They make love desperately, roughly, out of their deep need for connection with another human being. The relationship grows tentatively and increasingly tenderly, offering them – and us – a glimmer of hope, despite Leticia's discovery that Hank had been in charge of her husband's execution. This is not a comfortable film, but it is honest – about the potential difficulties of parent-child relationships, the destructive effects of racism, the impact of crime, the awfulness of capital punishment, the deep need for connection and love, and more besides. Johnston shows how such glimpses of fragile beauty in the midst of a broken, hopeless world echo the themes of Ecclesiastes. They are pointers, as is Ecclesiastes, to the fact that life has intimations of meaning within it, because of the way God has made us. They point beyond our circumstances to God himself, since there is only any meaning and any value if God really is there.

Secondly, and closely related to the question of whether or not the film is being truthful, we need to ask, does it raise the right questions? The answers we see on screen may be very inadequate, but it is vitally important to raise honest questions about life, which are often profound in their implications. *Collateral* (Michael Mann, 2004), for example, asks some important ethical questions yet presents little in the way of answers.

The third aspect of the ethical dimension is the obvious question of whether or not the morality we see portrayed on screen is consistent with biblical morality. Fourth, we need to ask what stance the movie is adopting towards the moral behaviour within it. That is, does it ultimately commend or condemn certain behaviour? How does this film suggest I should live? *About a Boy* (Chris and Paul Weitz, 2002), for example, shows Will (Hugh Grant) as a dissolute playboy who is utterly self-centred, rejoicing in his independence. Even his acts of kindness are done solely with the intention of attracting a woman. But by the end of the film he realises that he does, in fact, need real relationships rather than acquaintances and one-night stands. Life, he discovers, is about giving and receiving love. Ultimately, at least some of his immoral behaviour has been undermined.

The worldview level

Since the bulk of this book has been about understanding movies at the level of worldviews, I need say little more about it at this point, except to reinforce that it is vital that we do work at responding to films in this way.

As we saw in Chapter 2, we need to both celebrate the good and challenge the bad. There are aspects of virtually all films about which we can be positive (which is not to say that we can *commend* virtually all films). The more positive elements there are, the more sympathetic we are likely to feel to the movie as a whole. It is good to have plenty to be enthusiastic about, but we need to bear in mind that this could make us less alert to the areas of disagreement. We may thus fail to notice or be concerned by some other elements. The positive elements which may win our uncritical admiration for a movie may be nothing to do with the worldview, but may be emotional, born out of its sheer beauty and emotional weight. Think, for instance, of *The English Patient* (Anthony Minghella, 1996). The breathtaking cinematography, moving score and heartfelt emotion can cause us to overlook the immorality of the value system within the film, which includes infidelity, betrayal, treason and euthanasia. On the other hand, disagreeing with the worldview of a film should not stop us from praising other aspects of it (such as those we have already mentioned in this chapter). The point is to keep our critical faculties alert so that we are neither overly positive nor overly negative in our reactions. As we saw in Chapter 1, we always need to allow for both faces of reality – that which reflects God's image in humanity and that which reflects human rebellion.

It is only fair to point out, though, as I have already intimated, that learning to 'read' a film in this way can be hard work at first. But it is only through practice – and preferably by going through the learning experience with others – that it becomes a natural part of one's viewing. Do not expect to be able to walk straight out of the next movie you see and do a rigorous, in-depth analysis of the worldview. It may be a question of just spotting one or two things in each film to start with, but as you become more experienced, so you will find yourself seeing more. It is something which we can always keep on improving at since the nature of cinema is that we have to contend both with great complexity (even within a single film) as well as great diversity.

The spiritual level

Just as I reject the distinction between sacred and secular, I also want to reject the notion that some of life is spiritual, while some of it is not. All of life is spiritual in some sense, and all of it is to be done for God's glory.[12] As the early-twentieth-century theologian and Dutch Prime Minister Abraham Kuyper once said

No single piece of our mental world is to be hermetically sealed off from the rest, and there is not a square inch in the whole domain of our human existence over which Christ, who is Sovereign over all, does not cry: 'Mine!'[13]

However, we do also need to think about our spiritual growth in relation to the movies we see. As I have already noted, we are to walk a tightrope between engaging meaningfully with our culture and developing our holiness. It is relatively easy to identify that which is likely to make me fall off on the side of compromise, though it is harder to have the self-discipline not to do so. But spiritual growth is more than just a matter of not falling when we are tempted; it is also a question of being aware of weak points and actively working at developing in every area. Yes, movies can present images and ideas which have a negative effect on me, but they can both help me to see more clearly what I am like and can present images and ideas which can have a very positive impact. We can respond spiritually to films by identifying sinful aspects of ourselves, through seeing them lived out on screen perhaps, and repenting of them. And we can respond spiritually by determining to emulate positive values and characteristics we see on screen.

For example, in *Jerry Maguire* (Cameron Crowe, 1996), it is straightforward to identify the early focus on money. We can sagely shake our heads and say that life for a Christian is not about 'showing me the money', and feel self-satisfied that we have identified and rejected the temptation. But we must recognise that Rod Tidwell (Cuba Gooding Jr.) is concerned to get a good financial deal because he knows he cannot play football for much longer and he needs to provide for his family's future. Now it is a rather more subtle problem: that of justifying our materialism on the basis of providing for our family. The issues are those of self-justification and self-sufficiency rather than dependence on God, and of believing that we have the right to a standard of living comparable to our friends. Our quick reaction in condemning Rod may blind us to the fact that he has very similar values to us. Or what about Jerry (Tom Cruise) himself? He is hardworking, motivated and principled. But he is completely wrapped up in his work and Dorothy (Renée Zellweger) is neglected. This is not presented in any way in the movie as something which I might *want* to emulate, but it does hold up a mirror to many of us. We are hardworking, motivated, principled, yes. But also neglectful and, therefore, self-absorbed – whatever justifying gloss we may put on it. Dorothy, however, is inspired by what she sees as visionary leadership; she is self-sacrificing and committed to the work, but, more crucially, she is committed to Jerry himself. Eventually, Jerry is able to recognise just how important this relationship is, and echoes the words of the deaf person in the elevator from early in the film: 'You complete me.' That should in one sense be true of the partners in any marriage. At the same time, it can never be fully true because the function of marriage is to point us beyond human relationships to Jesus the Bridegroom. It is him who can ultimately complete each one of us. If I am responding at a spiritual level to *Jerry Maguire,* I will search my heart to see how self-obsessed I am, and look to work harder at my relationships both with my family and with God.

Another important aspect of responding spiritually to movies is that many films deliberately include religious motifs or ideas, or have examples of self-sacrifice which echo that of Jesus Christ in some way. In *The Iron Giant* (Brad Bird, 1999), the robot sacrifices himself and is miraculously resurrected. In *The Spitfire Grill* (Lee David Zlotoff, 1996), Percy Talbott (Alison Elliott) is an outsider who turns around a community and dies for the sake of someone else. Luke (Paul Newman) in *Cool Hand Luke* (Stuart Rosenberg, 1967) is a very deliberate Christ figure with echoes of his miracles, crucifixion and resurrection. Christ may be echoed in more ways than sacrifice or death, however: the way Ernesto (Ché) Guevara (Gael Garcîa Bernal) shakes hands with leprosy patients in *The Motorcycle Diaries* (Walter Salles, 2004) or the care and compassion of Sister Helen Prejean (Susan Sarandon) in *Dead Man Walking* (Tim Robbins, 1995). These ingredients may help us to understand more fully or see more clearly some aspect of Jesus' life and sacrifice, so moving us to be more grateful for our salvation and more determined to live in the light of it.

Helping Others to Respond

We also need to help others to respond to movies. With Christian friends, we need to encourage and enable them to respond in all the ways I have just outlined. By asking questions and prompting others to reflect on what they have seen and heard, we can help them to evaluate the emotional impact, moral integrity and worldview of the movie, and to identify implications for their own discipleship.

With friends who are not Christians, we need to do the same – except with a difference in emphasis. What a Christian sees as an implication for their personal discipleship could well be quite a challenge to the worldview of someone who is not a Christian. Indeed, discussing a movie at a worldview level is likely to result in some wonderfully interesting discussion. It is relatively easy to do this because people do not find movies threatening: going to watch a film and chatting about it afterwards is so much a part of normal life – and it is fun. It can be something that happens naturally as we watch and talk about films with our friends. But many people enjoy films so much that it is not difficult to suggest getting a small group together (a CultureWatch Group, for example[14]) to watch a film together and then talk about it. It does not need to be a profoundly spiritual film. In fact, I think it is possible to have good worldview-level conversations about almost any film. Some years ago I was chatting with an acquaintance, a very bright professor who was not a Christian, and he asked what films I had watched recently. Somewhat embarrassed, I confessed that I had needed to see *Spiceworld: The Movie* (Bob Spiers, 1997) – all in the cause of understanding the culture! He was surprised that there was anything of substance in it. I agreed, but suggested that this is the point of the film: image is everything. The film showed the Spice Girls as being young, fun and cool: people who love their music but don't take it or anything else seriously – not even themselves. We ended up having a long and stimulating conversation about our society's obsession with image and how nothing is taken seriously. We talked about hedonism, morality and the point of life – big issues that had never previously come up in our conversations. If it is possible to get onto those kinds of issues from such a lightweight film, imagine how much there would be to discuss after watching *O Brother, Where Art Thou?* (Joel Coen, 2000), *Dogville* (Lars von Trier, 2003), *On the Waterfront* (Elia Kazan, 1954), *Magnolia* (Paul Thomas Anderson, 1999) or anything by Robert Bresson, Ingmar Bergman or Carl Theodor Dreyer.[15]

Five Principles for Engaging with Movies

Finally, let me summarise with five key principles for

engaging with films. You will find a list of useful questions to consider when doing so, in Appendix 1.

1. Let films speak on their own terms

It is vitally important, as I hope has become clear throughout this book, to hear what the film is saying, not what we think it should be saying. Christians seem to have an unfortunate tendency to squeeze movies into a Christian framework and end up limiting their engagement with a film to spotting analogies with the gospel. Many well-meaning but naively uncritical Christians assumed that *The Matrix* was a Christian film when it was first released. But although there are many deliberate Christian allusions within it, the Wachowski Brothers are not Christians and they have interwoven many disparate ideas into their trilogy.[16]

2. Identify the themes

Work out what issues the film is dealing with and think about them at a worldview level. What does the film say about the issues, and how does this compare with a Christian perspective?

3. Keep asking questions

As I have commented several times, it is crucial to keep asking questions while we are watching films. By constantly questioning, we resist the temptation to make instant judgments on the worth of a film based on its genre, setting, aspects of its morality, links to the Christian faith, and so on. (See list of summary questions to ask about films in Appendix 1.)

While of course we want to encourage people to give serious consideration to the claims of Christ, it is best if this kind of discussion is genuinely open, exploring each other's different perspectives and beliefs since the truth can stand for itself. The best way to do this is by asking questions – and listening carefully to the responses. People can get understandably defensive when a Christian refuses to listen to another person's point of view but insists on explaining their own (sometimes at considerable length!).

4. Be positive but be clear

As I have reiterated several times already, we need to celebrate the good, but graciously challenge the bad. This means that we must maintain the biblical perspective of seeing human beings as rebellious image-bearers and the films they make as manifestations of both sides of human nature. As I commented in Chapter 2, we are looking for reflections of God's image: truth, insight, and sensitivity to the difficulties and tensions of life. We are looking for evidence of a deep longing for God. And we are looking for reflections of our rebellion: error, blindness and insensitivity. We are looking to see what has been substituted for God.

5. Be alert to the possibility of God's grace at work

Engaging with movies in this kind of way is very exciting – especially if you are able to do so with people who have other worldviews. But even more exciting is the discovery that God's grace is at work through it all. It may be at work in our lives as the Holy Spirit uses a film to enable us to see something that needs addressing in our lives, or encourages us in some way. God's grace may be at work in the lives of those with whom we chat about films. In fact, if we get to discuss big issues from a Christian perspective I would say that it is evidence that God's grace certainly is at work. God's grace may even be at work in the lives of the film-makers whose work we enjoy, enabling them to discover some truth, show human life in a particularly honest way, ask the right questions, or even to recognise that they need something beyond their own resources – enabling them to recognise that they need God. What could be more exciting than seeing God's grace at work?

Conclusion

Film is an exciting, engaging and potent medium, combining the age-old power of storytelling with the richness and complexity of image and sound. We are so familiar with many of the techniques of cinema that most of the time we barely need to think about them in order to understand a movie. But I believe passionately that if Christians are serious about engaging with culture as well as growing in holiness, we must thoughtfully consider the way films communicate their messages. It is important for our engagement that we are able to understand and identify with the culture in which we live so that, like Paul in Athens, we are able to communicate the good news of Jesus Christ clearly, relevantly and engagingly. It is important for us too, so that we do not unthinkingly absorb ideas and values which are inconsistent with God's words to us in the Bible. My longing is that we would no longer simply see films and other media as mere entertainment, letting it all wash over us without seriously thinking about it; but rather that we learn to love the Lord our God with all our heart, soul, strength *and* mind[17] while we are watching films. By doing so we can help ourselves and others to discover the truth of the greatest story the world has ever known.

Notes

1 Quoted in Jeremy S. Begbie, *Voicing Creation's Praise: Towards a Theology of the Arts* (Edinburgh: T&T Clark, 1991) p. 219.

2 Luke 10:27.

3 Martin Baker and Kate Brooks, *Knowing Audiences: Judge Dredd, Its Friends, Fans and Foes* (Luton: University of Luton Press, 1998) p. 149–150. Baker and Brooks' book is much more than a consideration of *Judge Dredd:* it is an entertaining and helpful consideration of the interaction of audiences with films.

4 At least until the electronic age when we discovered that gold is an extremely good conductor and is therefore ideal for use in electrical contacts.

5 Not everybody thinks so, of course. Steve Rose in *The Guardian* called it a 'nauseating scene' (17 September 2004 – arts.guardian.co.uk/fridayreview/story/0,12102,1306072,00.html).

6 Begbie, *Voicing Creation's Praise*, p. 224.

7 There has been considerable controversy over the historical honesty of both films, however. Those who criticise them on this count clearly do not see the films as excellent.

8 Remember that very non-realistic genres like fantasy or science fiction can be equally, or even more, truthful than films set in the 'real' world. Fantasy writer Ursula Le Guin wrote: 'For fantasy is true, of course. It isn't factual, but it is true. . . . They know that its truth challenges, even threatens, all that is false, all that is phoney, unnecessary,

and trivial in the life they have let themselves be forced into living.' (Ursula K. Le Guin, *The Language of the Night: Essays on Fantasy and Science Fiction*, second edition (New York: HarperCollins, 1992), p. 40.)

9 Gordon Matties, 'Recent Books on Faith & Film' – www.cmu.ca/faculty/gmatties/New%20Books%20on%20Film%20and%20Faith.htm.

10 Peter Fraser and Vernon Edwin Neal, *Reviewing the Movies: A Christian Response to Contemporary Film* (Wheaton, Ill.: Crossway, 2000) pp. 35–35.

11 Robert K. Johnston, *Useless Beauty: Ecclesiastes Through the Lens of Contemporary Film* (Grand Rapids, Mich.: Baker Academic, 2004).

12 See Colossians 3:17, for example.

13 James D. Bratt, *Abraham Kuyper: A Centennial Reader* (Grand Rapids, Mich.: Eerdmans, 1998) p. 488.

14 See www.damaris.org/culturewatchgroups/ for information.

15 The Top 100 Spiritually Significant Films list at www.artsandfaith.com/t100/ would make a good starting point. Filmography for this book available at www.damaris.org/focus

16 For a more detailed consideration of this issue within the *Matrix* trilogy, see my chapter 'Red Pill, Blue Pill' in Steve Couch (ed.), *Matrix Revelations: A Thinking Fan's Guide to the Matrix Trilogy* (Milton Keynes: Damaris, 2003) pp. 189–207.

17 Luke 10:27.

Appendix 1:

Questions to Consider When Watching a Film

The questions in this appendix are intended to help you organise your thinking as you watch a film, and also serves as a summary of the book. It is a long list – and it is still far from comprehensive. Clearly it is not something which can be memorised as a whole, but I would strongly recommend memorising the ten main headings to help you structure your thinking about a film while you are watching it, or while talking to friends about it afterwards. I would also urge you to learn the five key worldview questions (question 9 a–e below) as a framework for thinking about this vital aspect of films. As well as helping you in your own thinking about movies, these questions also provide a useful framework for group discussions (in a CultureWatch Group, for example). You can download a printable copy from www.damaris.org/focus/ as well as guidelines for leading discussions. Group discussions immediately after a film benefit significantly from ten minutes in which the members can reflect quietly on the film before sharing their thoughts with others. Extrovert members who like to do all their thinking aloud may be champing at the bit, but will still find it useful. Those who tend more towards intro-version will find this space of time invaluable.

1. Initial response

How did the film make you feel?
What aspect of the film did you most engage with?
What will you remember?
What does it make you think about?
Would you watch it again? Why/why not?
How would a second viewing be different? What would you focus on?
How would different people view this film differently (dependent on gender, age, ethnic background, world-view, etc.)?

2. What is the place of this film within the culture?

How popular is this film? How well did it do at the box office?
How influential is it? Has it been referenced in later films, television programmes, etc.?
What kind of buzz has it created? What media exposure has the film received? What has the critical response (reviews in newspapers, websites, etc.) been? Why?
How are cultural references (to history, books, films, music, etc.) used?
Is history treated fairly, or twisted to suit the film-makers' purposes?
If the film is an adaptation of earlier material, how faithful is it to the original? What changes have been made? Why?

3. How well has the film been made?

Is artistic and technical excellence achieved by screenplay, direction, cinematography, acting, editing, special effects, soundtrack, and so on?
What were the particular strengths and weaknesses?

a) Who are the film-makers? (See Chapter 4)

Who wrote the screenplay (and the original story if the film is an adaptation)?
Who directed and produced the film?
Do the writers and directors have a characteristic style or particular preoccupations? What does this tell you?
What do we know about the worldviews of these people – from their other work or from interviews?

b) Acting performances

What did you think of the casting?
What expectations were created by the use of particular actors?
Which performances particularly stood out?

4. What was the original context of the film? (See Chapter 3)

When was the film made? What was the prevailing worldview?
Does the film endorse this worldview or represent a challenge to it?

5. What is the genre? (See Chapter 6)

Is it fantasy, biography, drama, comedy, science fiction, historical drama, horror, romance, war, Western, romantic comedy, film noir, documentary, etc.?
What are the conventions of this genre?
How are genre conventions reinforced or subverted?

6. How is the narrative structured? (See Chapter 5)

What is the plot – what happens (in summary)?
When do the turning points in the narrative come? Are the major sections evenly balanced?

a) Consistency, cause and effect

Are the events in the story presented as a chain of cause and effect or are there unmotivated coincidences?
Does God have a role, or is there an impersonal force of fate?
Is the invented reality consistent?
If reality is inconsistent, is this because it is set in a dream or some other fantasy? Why? What does this communicate?
Is time linear or nonlinear?

b) Who is the protagonist?

Does the film feature single protagonist, dual protagonists (two sharing the same goals), parallel protagonists (two equally-balanced protagonists with opposing goals) or multiple protagonists?

How would you describe the protagonist(s) (active or passive, character, etc.)?

What are the protagonist(s) goals? Is there a time deadline?

What worldview is represented by the protagonist(s)?

c) *What is the force of antagonism?*

What problems are faced by the protagonist(s)?

How do these relate to the Fall?

Do the forces of antagonism represent a particular worldview?

d) *Who are the other characters?*

How would you describe them?

What worldview(s) do they represent?

What do they want?

Who is your favourite character? Why?

Which characteristic would you want to imitate?

e) *Consequences and change*

What choices do the characters make?

What other changes take place?

What motivates the choices and changes?

What are the consequences?

f) *How is resolution achieved?*

Is the ending closed or open?

Has there been any external change?

Are the problems resolved? How? If not, why not?

What self-discovery has the protagonist made?

How are the characters able to find the answers they need?

Does the film ultimately affirm or undercut the worldview it initially appears to support?

7. How is meaning created? (See Chapters 4 and 5)

a) Mise-en-scène

How is the film lit?

Is colour significant? If so, how?

Where is the camera for key shots? What angles does it shoot from?

How were long shots, close-ups, etc. used?

Whose point of view does the camera represent?

How did the sets, locations and props contribute to the meaning of the film?

How is our attention drawn to particular images?

Are there any recurring motifs?

Are there significant symbols and metaphors?

How else could key shots have been filmed – why did the director do it in this way?

b) Editing

What is the editing style?

How are non-standard edits (match cuts, dissolves, wipes, jump cuts, etc.) used?

Are there any particularly significant edits?

How does the editing contribute to the meaning of the film?

c) Soundtrack

What emotional effect did the soundtrack create?
Did any sound effects contribute to the meaning at any point?
How did the score enhance your understanding of scenes?

d) Titles

Was any important information given on title cards?
How did they affect your understanding of the film?

8. What are the key themes? (See Chapter 7)

Morality, politics, religion, sexuality, happiness, freedom, love, spirituality, identity, etc.
How does the theme develop and become clear?
How is the theme explored and emphasised?
Is the theme explored in fresh ways?
How do other films handle the theme?
Are there religious themes or connections? How is faith treated (if at all)?
Are there any echoes of Christ? If so, how are they dealt with?

9. What is the worldview? (See Chapter 2)

a) What is the view of reality?

Is the physical world all there is, or is there a spiritual dimension as well? Which is more important?
Why is the world like it is? Where did it come from?

What kind of god or gods are there, if any? If so, what are they like? Or is fate used as a substitute for God?

b) *What is the view of humanity?*

What are the distinctive things – if any – about human beings?
Where did we come from?
What happens when we die?
Is the film pessimistic or optimistic about human nature?
Do human beings have genuine freedom, or are they entirely subject to forces beyond their control?
Do characters show any evidence of spirituality?
What is the point of life?
Are some human beings more important than others?
Is community viewed as fractured and dysfunctional or united and nurturing?
What is the view of the family? How do families function?
Who is the butt of any humour? Why?

c) *What is the view of knowledge?*

How do characters know what is true – through experience, logic, intuition or revelation?
What is the film's view on these different ways of knowing?
How do the characters make decisions?
Where does wisdom come from?
Where does meaning come from?
What is the film's view of truth?

d) *What is the view of right and wrong?*

Is there any objective morality? Is there such a thing as good and evil?

How do characters know right and wrong?
Are the characters concerned primarily with the consequences of our actions, with ethical principles, or with being a good person?
What do the characters value?
What are the film's values – the attitudes toward truth, life, sex, family, community, etc.? Are these the same as the central characters' or different? Why?
What does goodness or beauty mean? How are they seen in the film?
Is there any judgement on wrong-doing?

e) What is the fundamental problem confronting all human beings, and what is the solution?

What is the basic problem which stops the characters being fulfilled? Is this seen as true for all humanity?
What do we most need in life?
What is the nature of evil? How can we be saved from it?

f) How well does the worldview measure up?

What do the film-makers want me to take away from this film?
Do the ideas *cohere?* (Do they hang together and make sense?) Which ones do and which do not?
Do the ideas work? What happens if you push them a little further? What kinds of tensions and difficulties would you run into? Where does it all come crashing down?
Do these ideas *correspond* with reality? Do they describe the world as it really is? Or are they a distortion, or even complete invention? Do they ignore some significant factor?

10. Truth, error and implications (see Chapters 2, 7 and 8)

What resonates with you? Why?

What truth or insight, error or blindness do you find in the film?

What aspects of the film are consistent or inconsistent with the Bible?

Is the film sensitive to the difficulties, dilemmas and tensions of life?

What else reflects the image of God in human beings?

How is human rebellion against God expressed?

Is there any evidence of the longing for God (a longing for peace)?

What substitutes for God does the film show?

'How might this film affect viewers as they return to their everyday activity? Will it inspire more hope and faith, or more despair? Will it encourage viewers to have courage, or will it inflame their fears? Will it inspire responsibility or recklessness?'[1]

Note

1 Jeffrey Overstreet, *Arts and Faith* discussion forum – artsandfaith.com/index.php?showtopic=10108.

Appendix 2:

The Problem of Content – Sex and Violence

In my early days working with Damaris, a member of my church was very concerned at my spiritual welfare because of 'all the dirty films' I had to watch. She was quickly reassured that such films were not the kind of material I was engaging with on a daily basis. However, she is far from the only one to raise misgivings like this – sometimes with rather less pastoral concern, such as the letter I received denouncing me as 'evil, unbiblical and foolish' for encouraging people to engage with the media at all. We have seen some of the biblical reasons for why I think engaging is important in Chapter 1 so I will not rehearse the arguments again here.[1] Relating to our culture does not mean exposing ourselves to the most offensive, depraved and godless material that is around. It *does* mean taking time to thoughtfully consider the films we are already watching and those that our friends are watching. For most of us, the vast majority of those films are mainstream rather than extreme.

However, there are still tough questions to be asked and issues to be addressed. The films which we and our friends watch may be mainstream, but we know all too well how the levels of sex, violence and offensive language have changed over recent years. Mainstream films contain plenty of it. These films may not be extreme, but they may nevertheless make us deeply uncomfortable. We can easily choose not to see a film that we expect will offend us, but what happens when our friends are going to see such a film? Should we stay away and make it clear why we do not want to go, or go with them for the sake of our friendship? What about those times when we are in the cinema and we discover that the film has content we were not expecting? How concerned should we be if we no longer notice swearing in films?

I do not think that there are any easy answers to these questions. But if we are serious about understanding the messages which are being communicated through movies, we will probably have to struggle with some questions and live with others. It is vital, first, that we put these things into a wider context.

Sins and Sensibilities

As I wrote in Chapter 1, all films – being the product of image-bearing rebels – reflect both the positive and negative aspects of human nature. Films, therefore, show all facets of human life including our sinfulness. Paul gives us some examples of sinful behaviour in Galatians 5 starting with 'sexual immorality, impurity [and] lustful pleasures' (v. 19, NLT). It is easy for us to identify these things as harmful in movies and to condemn those movies which contain them. But Paul continues his list with 'idolatry, sorcery, hostility, quarrelling, jealousy, outbursts of anger, selfish ambition, dissension, division, envy, drunkenness, wild parties and other sins like these' (vv. 20–21, NLT). The difficulty with these things is that we are surrounded by at least some of them virtually every day of our lives. Worse, if we are honest we recognise that such things live on in us.

In my experience, many Christians have finely tuned knee-jerk responses to a small number of issues which we feel are problematic: sex, violence, bad language and the occult. The presence of such things in a film can render the film unacceptable for us. Yet how much attention do we pay when we see selfish ambition portrayed on screen? We might well find Gordon Gekko (Michael Douglas) to be thoroughly objectionable in *Wall Street* (Oliver Stone, 1987), but how do we react to the protagonist Bud Fox (Charlie Sheen)? The likelihood is that we feel like we are on his side. We may consider that he makes some foolish decisions, but are we jumping up and down over his unbridled ambition? Most people would consider *Cars* (John Lasseter, 2006) to be good family entertainment, but again, Lightning McQueen is motivated by simple ambition. Is that not a problem? Or how about envy? It is probably not Jackie's envy of her sister (Emily Watson and Rachel Griffiths respectively) that we react to in *Hilary and Jackie* (Anand Tucker, 1998) but the infidelity. How many movies which include some of the sins from Paul's list have we seen without batting an eyelid? Peter Fraser comments, 'I have always been amazed at the selective Puritanism of so many Christians who find everything wrong with sins of the flesh but little wrong with sins like greed or gossip.'[2]

The Bible does not give us a table of sins ordered by their seriousness. In the Old Testament some are indicated as being more serious because they warrant capital punishment, but this includes dishonouring parents[3] – something which crops up in many films intended for children. In the New Testament, Paul gives another list of sins in Romans 1 (which, like the list in Galatians 5 is clearly intended to be representative rather than definitive) and comments that, 'those who do these things deserve to die, yet they do them anyway' (v. 32, NLT). *All* sin is rebellion against God, the ultimate moral authority of the universe, and therefore deserves nothing short of death – permanent separation from him. However, the Bible does highlight one sin again and again as being the most reprehensible of all. As I mentioned in Chapter 1, the most fundamental of all sins is idolatry – putting something other than God at the centre of our lives. It is something which Old Testament prophets rail against in no uncertain terms.[4] Christians may well notice and object to a film which endorses neo-paganism such as *The Craft* (Andrew Fleming, 1996) or *Practical Magic* (Griffin Dunne, 1998). But most of us seem to be blind to the biggest god of the western world: materialism. It is a central element in *Citizen Kane* (Orson Welles, 1941), *Gentlemen Prefer Blondes* (Howard Hawks, 1953) and *Jerry Maguire* (Cameron Crowe, 1996) among many others, and is part of the context for countless more. What do Christians worry about more with *Jerry Maguire* – Jerry's materialism or the swearing and sex? The tragedy is that we are so often blind to the materialism and consumerism in films because we, too, are infected with it. We, too, are idolaters.

It is absolutely vital to understand this broader perspective. Films raise many serious issues, and many different ways of sinning are presented to us as normal or attractive, yet Christians persist in ignoring most of these and reacting only to the usual suspects. These double standards make us think that sexual sin on screen is more serious than materialism or envy or outbursts of anger. It is not. All sin is a direct outworking of our rebellion against God; how we express that rebellion is, up to a point, neither here nor there. If we give children and young people the impression that only on-screen sex, violence and swearing matter, we are not equipping them to live effectively as Christians in a world in which they are surrounded by all kinds of sin.

However, I readily acknowledge that where the nature of the sin does begin to make a difference is in its impact on us and on those around us. If we are arrogant, it has an impact on our relationships – but that impact is cumulative. A display of arrogance one day is unlikely to have consequences that we must live with for years. Violence and sexual sin, though, are different matters. We are all tempted in some way, but to act on temptation by becoming violent with somebody or by engaging in extra-marital sexual activity can potentially have devastating and long-lasting consequences for our families and communities and for ourselves.

Biblical Models

A second problem with especially condemning sex and violence is that we seem to forget that the Bible itself is not afraid to deal with such issues. How can we say that these things are never justified in an artwork such as a film when they are found within the pages of the Bible itself? One of the most uncomfortable sermons I have ever had to preach was on Judges 17–21. These five chapters make for grim reading. They include accounts of theft, abduction, intimidation, violence, homosexuality, gang rape, genocide and revenge killing. There is plenty more violence in the Bible and some, like that in these chapters, is very explicit. Earlier in the book of Judges, for example, we read about Ehud plunging a sword into the belly of King Eglon so far that 'the handle disappeared beneath the king's fat. So Ehud did not pull out the dagger, and the king's bowels emptied.'[5]

There is sex, too, in the Bible: the Song of Songs, for example, is erotic Hebrew love poetry. It is rich with suggestive metaphors. The meaning of the garden metaphor, for instance, becomes a little clearer in the *New Living Translation's* rendering of 4:12–13:

> You are my private garden, my treasure, my bride, a secluded spring, a hidden fountain. Your thighs shelter a paradise of pomegranates with rare spices . . .

Again, the Bible gets very explicit, vulgar even, about sex at times – especially in the prophets. Ezekiel 16 and 23 are chapters in which Judah's unfaithfulness is described vividly as prostitution. Ezekiel's language is blunt and the imagery is graphic: 'At every street corner you built your lofty shrines and degraded your beauty, spreading your legs with increasing promiscuity to anyone who passed by. You engaged in prostitution with the Egyptians, your neighbours with large genitals, and aroused my anger with your increasing promiscuity.'[6] English translations are all rather polite and euphemistic in their rendering of these passages.

In Chapter 2 I noted William Romanowski's point that we cannot accuse God's own word of failing to meet the standard for our thinking set by Paul in Philippians 4:8. But just how are we to reconcile the two? Can such passages in Ezekiel be classed as 'pure and lovely and admirable'? It is hard to see how. But it is surely 'true and honourable and right' in the sense that it is a true indictment of Judah's waywardness. It is honourable because it upholds the honour of God by exposing the depths of human sin. It is a right announcement of judgement on the nation. In fact, it evokes the purity, loveliness and admirableness of God in sharp contrast to the depravity of human beings. It is not a question of the passage being comfortable and pleasant, but of it being true. Romanowski writes:

> The Bible does not excuse or overlook the evil it depicts. Even though the Bible explores the whole range of human depravity, the stories are always told with a certain perspective. The Bible shows evil and depravity as real, but also at odds with the best of human experience.[7]

If the Bible is to speak truthfully about the human condition – as it clearly does – then it seems that such things have a place within it. Art – including films – can also speak truthfully about the human condition, and there is, therefore, a place for sex and violence within it too. Fraser remarks:

> What Paul advocates in . . . Philippians 4:8, as applied to this topic, is not that we condemn violence and sexuality in art wherever it be found, but rather that we promote and dwell on art's positives – the good, true, noble and praise-worthy. . . . We need to avoid the tunnel vision that translates the Christian life into a set of 'do not' laws *and learn instead to live by redeeming every experience through the truth of Jesus Christ*.[8]

This last point is crucial. Why does the Bible contain incidents like those in the latter chapters of Judges? Paul writes that, 'These things happened to them as examples and were written down as warnings for us.'[9] He is specifically referring to some of the incidents during Israel's journey through the wilderness, but his point surely applies to the rest of Old Testament history. It seems that God in his wisdom thinks that we should know about the depths of human depravity.

Licence to Kill?

That raises an important question, however. Does the fact that the Bible includes these things imply that it is legitimate for film-makers to put whatever they like into their films, justifying it all as art reflecting life? Not at all. It *does* imply that we cannot condemn out of hand *any* inclusion of sexuality or violence, but that is not the same as condoning *every* instance of them. Fraser writes:

> The problem is not so much the presence of violence and sexuality in film; the problem is how and why the violence and sexuality are played out as they are. Unfortunately, here is where Christians need to think in terms of principles and not rules. Each film needs to be viewed according to its own special design.[10]

In other words, there are times when such things are absolutely vital to the story – and they need to be handled with great sensitivity by directors. How could Spielberg have made *Schindler's List* (1993) without including violence and nudity? Without being confronted with these realities we could not possibly begin to get a sense of the horror of it all. The nudity of the internees is not erotic, of course. But *Schindler's List* also contains two scenes of more erotic nudity – one involving Oskar Schindler (Liam Neeson) and the other involving Amon Goeth (Ralph Fiennes). In the first instance, it serves to show Schindler's character flaws, making clear that he was not an essentially good man who was inevitably going to help Jewish people. In the second, Goeth is also shown (in the same scene) using his rifle to shoot prisoners just for the fun of it. It communicates his utter depravity. The two incidents parallel each other, showing that both central characters had the same weakness for women. Now Spielberg could have shot these scenes differently, but he wanted a documentary feel to the film and therefore it had to be as naturalistic as possible. In the context I would see the violence and sexuality as being absolutely integral.

But there are, sadly, many times when directors fail to handle such material with sufficient sensitivity – or include plainly gratuitous incidents. Such things can mar otherwise fine films. We should neither allow them to blind us to the positive aspects of the film, nor allow the good things to blind us to the problems of inappropriate content. Barbara Nicolosi caught this balance well when she wrote about how she was both extremely impressed and disturbed by Todd Field's *Little Children* (2006):

> It's an amazing, thoughtful film that in so many ways reflects a profound Christian worldview. . . . Right there smack in the middle of all the wonder of it, this film has two or three fully nude absolutely graphic sex scenes. . . . the scenes are obscene in a way that wrecks the film by making part of it a thing of ugliness.[11]

All in the Cause of Art

A crucial part of our response to potentially offensive content is to consider it in the context of the film as a whole and its underlying worldview. Brian Godawa gives four aspects to consider in weighing up how appropriate the content is. The first is the intent of the film-makers. If the intention is to highlight the consequences of human wickedness then strong content may well be legitimate. *The Ice Storm* (Ang Lee, 1997) and *Unfaithful* (Adrian Lyne, 2002), for example, are about the destruction of lives and families as a consequence of adultery. However, the lingering shot of Halle Berry's breasts in *Swordfish* (Dominic Sena, 2001) is entirely without justification within the plot. It was rumoured that the scene was included simply to boost box office takings, though Warner Brothers and Berry denied it.

The second aspect Godawa highlights is the actual depiction of sex or violence. Is it just enough to make the point, or does it go too far? The sex scene in *Monster's Ball* (Marc Forster, 2001) is crucial to the development of the characters and their relationship. The scene makes clear that sex is forging a connection between these two broken people, and the roughness of it is an indicator of the depth of their need. But there is at least one shot that is far too explicit and seems unnecessary. What further purpose does it fulfil? It passes from essential plot and character development to voyeurism.

Some directors, like Quentin Tarantino trick us into thinking we see more than we do:

> His skill lies in coaxing the audience into thinking they are seeing gruesome violence without it actually happening on screen. A true cineaste, his

control of the viewers' imagination conjures up
infinitely more terrible scenes than anything the
camera can show them.[12]

Third, we need to look to the consequences. I have
discussed the importance of paying attention to consequences already in Chapter 5, but note the importance of
the moral aspect to this. The results of certain behaviour
are important within the narrative and for considering
the worldview, but it also enables us to make a judgement
about whether a director was right or wrong to include
particular scenes. When the daughter of Jimmy Markum
(Sean Penn) is found murdered in *Mystic River* (Clint
Eastwood, 2003), suspicions fall on his childhood friend
Dave (Tim Robbins). Jimmy takes the law into his own
hands in a brutal fashion – and the consequences are
terrible. Is the violence within the film appropriate?
Given the way the story develops, I would argue that it
is. Without it the power of the film would be lost.

Fourthly, we must consider the context. In some films,
the scenes of immoral behaviour are portrayed as such.
The affair between the two principal characters (Jeremy
Irons and Juliette Binoche) in *Damage* (Louis Malle, 1992)
is presented to us as immoral from the start. The sex
scenes show how they are completely taken over by their
sexual urges regardless of anything else. They are
arguably more graphic than they need to be, but this
could probably not be conveyed through metaphors or
symbols like a trail of clothes across the floor. We need to
understand how out of control they are – and the
consequences that follow. The drug-abusing context of
some shocking scenes in *Trainspotting* (Danny Boyle,
1996) makes their inclusion vital for us to begin to
understand that world. On the other hand, a film like

Lock, Stock and Two Smoking Barrels (Guy Ritchie, 1998) simply seems to indulge in violence for its own sake.

Context also relates to the intended audience. A movie like *American Pie* (Paul Weitz, 1999) is aimed squarely at teenagers – and that makes its sexual content inappropriate. It is not that films for teenagers should not deal with sex in some way. Quite the opposite in many ways, since the transition from childhood through puberty to sexual maturity is what makes that age such a big deal. But a responsible way of dealing with the subject is not to indulge in the exploits of four boys who are desperate to lose their virginity before they leave school. On the other hand, *Requiem for a Dream* (Darren Aronofsky, 2000) is clearly for an adult audience with its subject matter of drug-induced self-destruction. In its portrayal of the lengths to which a woman would go in order to get her next fix, the inclusion of some (though not all, in my opinion) sexual content was necessary and deeply distressing.

Watching What We Watch

While I do believe that it is legitimate for directors to include scenes that are shocking and will be offensive to some viewers, I am at the same time deeply disturbed by the constant pushing of moral boundaries. It means that directors find it ever easier to take the easy road of showing everything as it is rather than implying it. Art has always been able to suggest things to our vivid imaginations without necessarily showing us something explicitly, but there is less need for film-makers to even consider ways of avoiding being graphic. Since Michelangelo Antonioni's *Blow Up* first brought full-frontal nudity to British cinema screens in 1966, we have moved a long way. In 2004, Michael Winterbottom's *9 Songs* showed explicit scenes of unsimulated sex. What good has that done for any of us? Back in 1967 George Steiner wrote about the impoverishing effect which the explicit presentation of sex has on our imaginations:

> Future historians may come to characterize the present era in the West as one of a massive onslaught on human privacy, on the delicate processes by which we seek to become our own singular selves, to hear the echo of our specific being. . . .
>
> Sexual relations are, or should be, one of the citadels of privacy, the nightplace where we must be allowed to gather the splintered, harried elements of our consciousness to some kind of inviolate order and repose. . . . [Pornographers] subvert this last, vital privacy; they do our imagining for us. They take away the words that were of the night and shout them over the roof-tops, making them hollow. . . . Our dreams are marketed wholesale. . . . It is not a new freedom that they bring, but a new servitude.[13]

But while we may – and should – lament this decline in standards, the more immediate question is how we live in the world as it is now, and how we relate to the films that are around us. It comes back to the difficult balancing act I discussed in Chapter 1. How do we stay on the tightrope, avoiding a complete rejection of culture on the one hand, and an unthinking embrace of it on the other? How do we engage with our world and yet maintain our holiness?

I believe that a more rounded perspective on sex and violence is much more helpful than a knee-jerk response to every instance of it. As we have seen, understanding that these are not the only sins, that they are found in the Bible, and that there are times when they are artistically justifiable, helps us to be more integrated as Christians. Otherwise we end up denying certain facets of human existence and of the Bible itself. Within the context of this book about film and worldviews, it is also important to understand that we can and should approach films for understanding as much as for entertainment. That significantly helps us approach potentially troubling scenes with a greater distance, more objectively, rather than allowing them to sweep us along emotionally. Learning to think hard and critically about such things strengthens our moral muscles rather than weakens them. Paul writes:

> Take no part in the worthless deeds of evil and darkness; instead, expose them. It is shameful even to talk about the things that ungodly people do in secret. But their evil intentions will be exposed when the light shines on them, for the light makes everything visible.[14]

Christians often focus on the shamefulness of even talking about what ungodly people do in secret. But the context clearly shows that such things are to be exposed so that the light of God's truth may shine on them, showing them up for what they are. As we have already seen, the Bible itself talks about the things ungodly people do in secret. It is shameful, but the reality of human rebellion is, and it is something we must be frank about. But crucially, as we expose 'the worthless deeds of evil and darkness', we are not to take part in them. We sometimes do need to talk about them, and their portrayal in films, but we do not imitate them.

This is never to be used as an excuse for indulging our sinful natures. We are to stay on the tightrope, and not make engaging with culture into an excuse for falling off it. We need to know our own weaknesses and the temptations to which we are particularly prone. Then we need to be very careful about what we watch, while recognising that others may struggle with different issues and must make their own decisions.[15] We cannot and should not avoid every film that may contain something offensive in it, but we absolutely must keep ourselves in check, ensuring that we are concerned for our personal godliness, as well as for those around us to come to see the transformation which the gospel offers. Paul urges us to:

Keep a close watch on how you live and on your teaching. Stay true to what is right for the sake of your own salvation and the salvation of those who hear you.[16]

Notes

1 For a more detailed discussion of this, see my chapter 'A biblical perspective' in Nick Pollard; Paul Harris; Tony Watkins and Phil Wall, *Beyond the Fringe: Reaching People Outside the Church* (Leicester: IVP, 1999) pp. 86–98.

2 Peter Fraser and Vernon Edwin Neal, *ReViewing the Movies: A Christian Response to Contemporary Film* (Wheaton, Ill.: Crossway, 2000) p. 69.

3 Exodus 21:17.

4 See Isaiah 41:21–29 or Jeremiah 2, for example.

5 Judges 3:22 (NLT).

6 Ezekiel 16:25–26.

7 Romanowski, William D., *Eyes Wide Open: Looking for God in Popular Culture* (Grand Rapids, Mich.: Brazos Press, 2001) p. 124.

8 Fraser and Neal, *ReViewing the Movies*, p. 69 (my italics).

9 1 Corinthians 10:11.

10 Fraser and Neal, *ReViewing the Movies*, p. 67.

11 Barbara Nicolosi, '*Little Children* – Incredible, Thoughtful and Obscene', *Church of the Masses*, 9 October 2006 – churchofthemasses.blogspot.com/2006/10/little-children-incredible-thoughtful.html.

12 Wensley Clarkson, *Quentin Tarantino: Shooting from the Hip* (London: Piatkus, 1995) p. xix–xx.

13 George Steiner, *Language and Silence* (London: Faber & Faber, 1967) p. 97–99.

14 Ephesians 5:10–14 (NLT).

15 See 1 Corinthians 6:12; 8:9; 10:23.

16 1 Timothy 4:16 (NLT).

Bibliography

Andrew, Geoff, *Directors A–Z: A Concise Guide to the Art of 250 Great Film-Makers* (London: Prion, 1999).

Arroyo, José (ed.), *Action/Spectacle Cinema* (London: BFI, 2000).

Baker, Martin and Brooks, Kate, *Knowing Audiences: Judge Dredd, Its Friends, Fans and Foes* (Luton: University of Luton Press, 1998).

Barsotti, Catherine M. and Johnston, Robert K., *Finding God in the Movies: 33 Films of Reel Faith* (Grand Rapids, Mich.: Baker Books, 2004).

Barthes, Roland, *Image, Music, Text*, trans. Stephen Heath (London: Fontana, 1977 repr. 1993).

Basinger, Jeanine, *A Woman's View: How Hollywood Spoke to Women, 1930–1960* (Hanover, NH.: Wesleyan University Press, 1993).

Beard, William, *The Artist as Monster: The Films of David Cronenberg* (Toronto: University of Toronto Press, 2005).

Begbie, Jeremy S., *Voicing Creation's Praise: Towards a Theology of the Arts* (Edinburgh: T&T Clark, 1991).

Bellour, Robert, *The Analysis of Film* (Bloomington, Ind.: Indiana University Press, 2000).

Benjamin, Walter, 'The Work of Art in the Age of Mechanical Reproduction' – bid.berkeley.edu/bidclass/readings/benjamin.html.

Booker, Christopher, *The Seven Basic Plots: Why We Tell Stories* (London: Continuum, 2004).

Boorman, John (ed.), *Projections 4: Film-makers on Film-making* (London: Faber and Faber, 1994).

—— *Projections 5: Film-makers on Film-making* (London: Faber and Faber, 1996).

—— *Projections 6: Film-makers on Film-making* (London: Faber and Faber, 1996).

—— *Projections 7: Film-makers on Film-making* (London: Faber and Faber, 1997).

—— and Donohoe, Walter (eds.), *Projections 8: Film-makers on Film-making* (London: Faber and Faber, 1998).

Bordwell, David, *Making Meaning: Inference and Rhetoric in the Interpretation of Cinema* (Cambridge, Mass.: Harvard University Press, 1989).

—— *The Way Hollywood Tells It: Story and Style in Modern Movies* (Berkeley and Los Angeles: University of California Press, 2006).

—— and Thompson, Kristin, *Film History: An Introduction* (New York: McGraw-Hill, 1994).

—— —— *Film Art: An Introduction,* sixth edition (New York: McGraw-Hill, 2001).

—— —— and Staiger, Janet, *The Classical Hollywood Cinema: Film Style and Mode of Production to 1960* (London: Routledge, 1988).

Bratt, James D., *Abraham Kuyper: A Centennial Reader* (Grand Rapids, Mich.: Eerdmans, 1998).

Braudy, Leo and Cohen, Marshall (eds.), *Film Theory and Criticism,* sixth edition (New York: Oxford University Press, 2004).

Buñuel, Luis, *My Last Sigh* (New York: Alfred A. Knopf, 1983).

Burnett, David, *Clash of Worlds: What Christians Can Do in a World of Cultures in Conflict,* second edition (London: Monarch, 2002).

Buscombe, Edward, *Cinema Today* (London: Phaidon, 2003).

Cahoone, Lawrence E., *From Modernism to Postmodernism: An Anthology* (Oxford and Cambridge, Mass.: Blackwell, 1996).

Campbell, Joseph, *The Hero With a Thousand Faces* (New York: Pantheon Books, 1949).

Carroll, Noël, *Engaging the Moving Image* (New Haven: Yale University Press, 2003).

Carson, D.A., 'Three Books on the Bible: A Critical Review', *Reformation 21*, May 2006 – www.reformation21.com/Past_Issues/May_2006/Shelf_Life/Shelf_Life/181/vobId__29 26/pm__434/.

Caughie, John, *Theories of Authorship: A Reader* (London: Routledge, 1981).

Cawkwell, Tim, *The Filmgoer's Guide to God* (London: Darton, Longman and Todd, 2004).

Christianson, Eric S.; Francis, Peter; Telford, William R. (eds.), *Cinéma Divinité: Religion, Theology and the Bible in Film* (London: SCM Press, 2005).

Clarkson, Wensley, *Quentin Tarantino: Shooting from the Hip* (London: Piatkus, 1995).

Collins, Jim; Radner, Hilary and Collins, Ava Preacher (eds.), *Film Theory Goes to the Movies* (New York and London: Routledge, 1993).

Cook, Pam and Dodd, Philip, *Women and Film: A Sight and Sound Reader* (London: Scarlet Press, 1993).

Cook, Pam and Bernink, Mieke (eds.), *The Cinema Book*, second edition (London: British Film Institute, 1999).

Couch, Steve (ed.), *Matrix Revelations: A Thinking Fan's Guide to the Matrix Trilogy* (Milton Keynes: Damaris, 2003).

—— Williams, Peter S. and Watkins, Tony, *Back in Time: A Thinking Fan's Guide to Doctor Who* (Milton Keynes: Damaris, 2005).

Cousins, Mark, *The Story of Film* (London: Pavilion, 2004).

Couvares, Francis G. (ed.), *Movie Censorship and American Culture* (Washington: Smithsonian Institute Press, 1996).

Cronenberg, David, 'Acts Of Violence' (featurette), *A History of Violence* (Entertainment in Video, 2006).

Dahle, Lars, *Acts 17:16–34 – An Apologetic Model Then and Now?* (Doctoral thesis, Open University, 2001).

Deveney, Tristan, 'Chris Weitz Interview', *BridgeToTheStars.net*,

2004 – www.bridgetothestars.net/index.php?p=weitzinterview.

Eckman, James P., *The Truth About Worldviews: A Biblical Understanding of Worldview Alternatives* (Wheaton, Ill.: Crossway, 2004).

Elsaesser, Thomas with Wedel, Michael (eds.), *The BFI Companion to German Cinema* (London: British Film Institute, 1999).

Erickson, Glenn, 'Savant Review: The Man With No Name Trilogy', *DVDTalk.com*, 4 November 1999 – www.dvdtalk.com/dvdsavant/s90leonerev.html.

Evans, Peter William and Deleyto, Celestino, *Term of Endearment: Hollywood Romantic Comedy of the 1980s and 1990s* (Edinburgh: Edinburgh University Press, 1998).

Ford, Hamish, 'Ingmar Bergman', *Senses of Cinema*, November 2002 – www.sensesofcinema.com/contents/directors/02/bergman.html.

Fraser, Peter and Neal, Vernon Edwin, *ReViewing the Movies: A Christian Response to Contemporary Film* (Wheaton, Ill.: Crossway, 2000).

Gay, Craig, *The Way of the (Modern) World or, Why It's Tempting to Live As if God Doesn't Exist* (Carlisle: Paternoster, 1998).

Gazetas, Aristides, *An Introduction to World Cinema* (Jefferson, NC: McFarland, 2000).

Godawa, Brian, *Hollywood Worldviews: Watching Films with Wisdom and Discernment* (Downers Grove, Ill.: IVP, 2002).

Grant, Barry Keith (ed.), *Film Genre Reader II* (Austin, Tex.: University of Texas Press, 1995).

Green, Jonathon, *The Cassell Dictionary of Cynical Quotations* (London: Weidenfeld and Nicolson, 1994).

Hanson, Curtis, 'Off the Record' (featurette), *L.A. Confidential* (Warner Home Video, 1997).

Harris, Ed, 'Arts of Violence' featurette on *A History of Violence* DVD (Entertainment in Video, 2006).

Hawking, Stephen, *Black Holes and Baby Universes* (London: Bantam Press, 1993).

Hayward, Susan, *Cinema Studies: The Key Concepts*, second edition (Oxford: Routledge, 2000).

Hennigan, Adrian, 'Roger Michell', *BBC.co.uk* – www.bbc.co.uk/films/2004/11/25/roger_michell_enduring_love_interview.shtml.

Hennigan, Adrian, 'Getting Direct with Directors . . . No. 5: Roger Michell', *BBC Movies – Calling the Shots* – www.bbc.co.uk/films/callingtheshots/roger_michell.shtml.

Hibbs, Thomas S., *Shows About Nothing: Nihilism in Popular Culture from The Exorcist to Seinfeld* (Dallas: Spence, 1999).

Higgins, Gareth, *How Movies Helped Save My Soul: Finding Spiritual Fingerprints in Culturally Significant Films* (Lake Mary, Fla.: Relevant, 2003).

Hill, John and Church Gibson, Pamela, *The Oxford Guide to Film Studies* (Oxford: Oxford University Press, 1998).

Hirsch, Foster, *Love, Sex, Death and the Meaning of Life: The Films of Woody Allen*, second edition (Cambridge, Mass.: Da Capo, 2001).

Jackson, Kevin, *The Language of Cinema* (Manchester: Carcanet, 1998).

Jencks, Charles, *The Language of Post-Modern Architecture* (New York: Rizzolli, 1977).

Johnson, Steven, *Everything Bad is Good for You* (London: Allen Lane, 2005).

Johnston, Robert K., *Reel Spirituality* (Grand Rapids, Mich.: Baker Books, 2000).

—— *Useless Beauty: Ecclesiastes Through the Lens of Contemporary Film* (Grand Rapids, Mich.: Baker Academic, 2004).

Kabir, Nasreen Munni, *Bollywood, the Indian Cinema Story* (London: Channel 4, 2001).

Kael, Pauline, *I Lost it at the Movies: Film Writings 1954–1965* (New York: Marion Boyars, 1994).

Katz, Ephraim, *The Macmillan International Film Encyclopedia*, rev. Fred Klein and Ronald Dean Nolen (London: Macmillan, 2001).

Kaveney, Roz, *Teen Dreams: Reading Teen Film and Television from Heathers to Veronica Mars* (London and New York: I.B. Tauris, 2006).

Keller, Tim, 'A Biblical Theology of the City', *Evangelicals Now*,

July 2002 – www.e-n.org.uk/1869-A-biblical-theology-of-the-city.htm.

Kieslowski, Krzysztof, 'Under Kieslowski's Microscope' (featurette), *The Three Colours Trilogy* (Artificial Eye, 2004).

Kolker, Robert Philip, *A Cinema of Loneliness: Penn, Stone, Kubrick, Scorsese, Spielberg, Altman*, third edition (Oxford and New York: Oxford University Press, 2000).

Konigsberg, Ira, *The Complete Film Dictionary*, second edition (London: Bloomsbury, 1997).

Kupfer, Joseph H., *Visions of Virtue in Popular Film* (Boulder, Col. and Oxford: Westview, 1999).

Le Guin, Ursula K., *The Language of the Night: Essays on Fantasy and Science Fiction*, second edition (New York: HarperCollins, 1992).

Lumet, Sidney, *Making Movies* (New York: Vintage, 1995).

Lyon, David, *Postmodernity*, second edition (Buckingham: Open University, 1999).

Lyotard, Jean-François, *The Postmodern Condition: A Report on Knowledge*, trans. Geoff Bennington and Brian Massumi (Minneapolis: University of Minnesota Press, 1984) first published as *La condition postmoderne: rapport sur le savoir* (Paris: Éditions de Minuit, 1979).

MacDonald, Alan, *Movies in Close-Up: Getting the Most from Film and Video*, (Leicester: IVP, 1992).

Macnab, Geoffrey, *Key Moments in Cinema: The History of Film and Film-makers* (London: Hamlyn, 2001).

Marsh, Clive, *Cinema and Sentiment: Film's Challenge to Theology* (Milton Keynes and Waynesboro, Ga.: Paternoster, 2004).

—— and Ortiz, Gaye W., *Explorations in Theology and Film: Movies and Meaning* (Oxford: Blackwell, 1997).

Maslow, Abraham, *Motivation and Personality*, second edition (New York and London: Harper and Row, 1970).

Matties, Gordon, 'Recent Books on Faith & Film' – www.cmu.ca/faculty/gmatties/New%20Books%20on%20Film%20and%20Faith.htm.

—— 'What do movies do?' – www.cmu.ca/faculty/gmatties/What%20do%20movies%20do.htm.

McGrath, Alister, *Bridge-Building: Effective Christian Apologetics* (Leicester: IVP, 1992).

McKee, Robert, *Story: Substance, Structure, Style, and the Principles of Scriptwriting* (London: Methuen, 1999).

Miles, Margaret R., *Seeing and Believing: Religion and Values in the Movies* (Boston: Beacon Press, 1996).

Monaco, James, *How to Read a Film: Movies, Media, Multimedia*, third edition (New York and Oxford: Oxford University Press, 2000).

Mulvey, Laura, *Death 24X a Second: Stillness and the Moving Image* (London: Reaktion Books, 2005).

Murch, Walter, *In the Blink of an Eye: A Perspective on Film Editing* (Beverly Hills, Calif.: Silman-James, 1995).

Naugle, David, *Worldview: The History of a Concept* (Grand Rapids, Mich.: Eerdmans, 2002).

Nicolosi, Barbara, '*Little Children* – Incredible, Thoughtful and Obscene', *Church of the Masses*, 9 October 2006 – church of the masses.blogspot.com/2006/10/little – children – incredible – thoughtful.html.

Norris, Michelle, 'Behind the Scenes with Film Editor Walter Murch', *NPR* – www.npr.org/templates/story/story. php? storyId =4994411.

Nottingham, Stephen, 'The French New Wave' – ourworld.compuserve.com/homepages/Stephen_Nottingham/cintxt2.htm.

Orr, John, *Cinema and Modernity* (Cambridge: Polity, 1993).

Overstreet, Jeffrey, *Through a Screen Darkly: Looking Closer at Beauty, Truth and Evil in the Movies* (Ventura, Calif.: Regal, 2007).

Pearcey, Nancy, *Total Truth: Liberating Christianity from Its Cultural Captivity* (Wheaton, Ill.: Crossway, 2004).

Pearson, Roberta E. and Simpson, Philip (eds.), *Critical Dictionary of Film and Television Theory* (London: Routledge, 2001).

Pilkington, Ed, 'A History of Violence', *The Guardian*, 6 October 2006 – film.guardian.co.uk/interview/interviewpages/0,,1888375,00.html.

Pinsky, Mark I., *The Gospel According to Disney* (Louisville, Ky.: Westminster John Knox, 2004).

Pollard, Nick, *Evangelism Made Slightly Less Difficult* (Leicester: IVP, 1997).

—— Harris, Paul; Watkins, Tony and Wall, Phil, *Beyond the Fringe: Reaching People Outside the Church* (Leicester: IVP, 1999).

—— and Couch, Steve, *Get More Like Jesus While Watching TV* (Milton Keynes: Damaris, 2005).

Prince, Stephen (ed.), *Screening Violence* (New Brunswick, NJ: Rutgers University Press, 2000).

Puntis, Caroline, 'Mulholland Dr.', *CultureWatch*, 2004 – www.damaris.org/content/content.php?type=5&id=347.

Ricoeur, Paul, *Freud and Philosophy: An Essay on Interpretation* (New Haven: Yale University Press, 1970).

Robson, Eddie, *Coen Brothers* (London: Virgin, 2003).

Romanowski, William D., *Eyes Wide Open: Looking for God in Popular Culture* (Grand Rapids, Mich.: Brazos Press, 2001).

Rose, Steve, 'The Shawshank Redemption', *The Guardian*, 17 September 2004 – arts.guardian.co.uk/fridayreview/story/0,12102,1306072,00.html.

Sargeant, Amy, *British Cinema: A Critical History* (London: BFI, 2005).

Sartre, Jean-Paul, 'Existentialism is a Humanism', 1946 – www.marxists.org/reference/archive/sartre/works/exist/sartre.htm.

Sartre, Jean-Paul, *Being and Nothingness*, trans. Hazel Barnes (New York: Simon & Schuster, 1956) first published as *L'Être et le Néaut* (Paris: Gallimard, 1943).

Scalzi, John, *The Rough Guide to Sci-Fi Movies* (London: Rough Guides, 2005).

Scorsese, Martin and Wilson, Michael Henry, *A Personal Journey with Martin Scorsese Through American Movies* (London: Faber and Faber, 1997).

Silver, Alain and Ursini, James, *Film Noir* (Köln and London: Taschen, 2004).

Sim, Stuart (ed.), *The Icon Critical Dictionary of Postmodern Thought* (Cambridge: Icon, 1998).

Sire, James W., *How to read slowly: reading for comprehension,* second edition (Wheaton, Ill.: Harold Shaw, 1989).

—— *Naming the Elephant: Worldview as a Concept* (Downers Grove, Ill.: IVP, 2004).

—— *The Universe Next Door: A Basic Worldview Catalog,* fourth edition (Downers Grove, Ill.: IVP, 2004).

Slocum, J. David (ed.), *Violence and American Cinema* (New York: Routledge, 2001).

Stam, Robert, *Film Theory: An Introduction* (Oxford: Blackwell, 2000).

—— and Raengo, Alessandra, *A Companion to Literature and Film* (Oxford: Blackwell, 2004).

Steiner, George, *Language and Silence* (London: Faber & Faber, 1967).

Stone, Bryan P., *Faith and Film: Theological Themes at the Cinema* (St. Louis, Mo.: Chalice Press, 2000).

Tasker, Yvonne (ed.), *Action and Adventure Cinema* (Abingdon: Routledge, 2004).

Thompson, Kristin, *Storytelling in the New Hollywood: Understanding Classical Narrative Technique* (Cambridge, Mass.: Harvard University Press, 1999).

Thomson, David, *The New Biographical Dictionary of Film* (London: Little, Brown, 2002).

Tompkins, Jane, *West of Everything: The Inner Life of Westerns* (Oxford: Oxford University Press, 1992).

Truffaut, François, 'Une Certaine Tendance du Cinéma Français', *Cahiers du Cinema,* No. 31, January 1954.

UNESCO (United Nations Educational, Scientific and Cultural Organization) Universal Declaration on Cultural Diversity, 21 February 2002 – www.unesco.org/education/imld_2002/unversal_decla.shtml.

Vogler, Christopher, *The Writer's Journey* (London: Pan, 1998).

Voytilla, Stuart, *Myth and the Movies: Discovering the Mythic Structure of Over 50 Unforgettable Films* (Studio City, Calif: Michael Wiese Productions, 1999).

Walker, John, *Halliwell's Film, Video and DVD Guide 2006* (London: HarperCollins Entertainment, 2005).

Walsh, Brian J. and Middleton, Richard J., *The Transforming Vision: Shaping a Christian Worldview* (Downers Grove, Ill.: IVP, 1984).

Watkins, Tony, *Dark Matter: A Thinking Fan's Guide to Philip Pullman* (Milton Keynes: Damaris, 2004).

—— (ed.), *Sex and the Cynics: Talking About the Search for Love* (Milton Keynes: Damaris, 2005).

—— *Truth Wars: Talking About Tolerance* (Milton Keynes: Damaris, 2005).

—— *Playing God: Talking About Ethics in Medicine and Technology* (Milton Keynes: Damaris, 2006).

—— *Spooked: Talking About the Supernatural* (Milton Keynes: Damaris, 2006).

Wilkens, Steve and Padgett, Alan G., *Christianity and Western Thought: A History of Philosophers, Ideas and Movements, Volume 2: Faith and Reason in the Nineteenth Century* (Downers Grove, Ill.: IVP, 2000).

Williams, Linda Ruth and Hammond, Michael, *Contemporary American Cinema* (London and Boston: Open University Press, 2006).

Winter, Bruce, 'On Introducing Gods to Athens: An Alternative Reading of Acts 17:18–20', *Tyndale Bulletin*, Vol. 47 No. 1, 1996, p. 72.

Witcombe, Christopher L.C.E., 'Art and Artists: The Roots of Modernism' – witcombe.sbc.edu/modernism/roots.html.

Wolterstorff, Nicholas, *Art in Action* (Grand Rapids, Mich.: Eerdmans, 1980).

Wright, N.T., *The New Testament and the People of God* (London: SPCK, 1992).

Zee-Jotti, Marco, 'Bringing Up Daddy', *Filmwaves*, Issue 30, Winter 2006, pp. 14–15.

Žižek, Slavoj (ed.), *Everything You Always Wanted to Know About Lacan (But Were Afraid to Ask Hitchcock)* (London and New York: Verso, 1992).

Some useful websites

There are links to these sites and others at
www.damaris.org/focus.

Damaris Trust: the portal to all the Damaris sites –
www.damaris.org

CultureWatch: hundreds of articles and study guides on films,
books, television and music – www.culturewatch.org

Arts and Faith Forum: very active discussion forums on all aspects
of the relationship between the arts and Christian faith with a
strong emphasis on film – www.artsandfaith.com

Bright Lights Film Journal: wide-ranging collection of reviews,
articles and interviews – www.brightlightsfilm.com

Film-Philosophy: articles about films and film-making from a
philosophical perspective – www.film-philosophy.com

Journal of Religion and Film: online academic journal with
scholarly articles exploring film in relation to theology and
philosophy – www.unomaha.edu/jrf

Masters of Cinema: articles on world cinema, primarily focusing
on directors like Andrei Tarkovsky, Carl Theodor Dreyer
and Robert Bresson – www.mastersofcinema.org

Senses of Cinema: wide-ranging collection of articles about great
directors and films – www.sensesofcinema.com

Index

About the Author

Tony Watkins spent several years teaching physics and mathematics in a girls' school before joining the Universities and Colleges Christian Fellowship (UCCF) as a staff worker in the south of England. He joined The Damaris Project (the precursor to the Damaris Trust) as Project Co-ordinator when it was launched in 1996.

Since the formation of The Damaris Trust in 2000 he has been Managing Editor of CultureWatch (a Damaris website which engages with the media from a Christian perspective for a secular readership), as well as heading up the Damaris workshop programme and CultureWatch groups. Tony is the author of *Dark Matter: A Thinking Fan's Guide to Philip Pullman*, the co-author of *Back In Time: A Thinking Fan's Guide to Doctor Who*, and contributed chapters to *Matrix Revelations: A Thinking Fan's Guide to the Matrix Trilogy*. He is also the editor of the *Talking About* series of books and was part of the writing team for Damaris's popular *Connect Bible Studies* series from 2001 to 2004.

Tony and his wife, Jane, have three boys, Charlie, Oliver and Philip, and live in Southampton.

Other Titles from Damaris Books

Back In Time: A Thinking Fan's Guide to Doctor Who
   by Steve Couch, Tony Watkins and Peter S. Williams

Dark Matter: A Thinking Fan's Guide to Philip Pullman
   by Tony Watkins

Matrix Revelations: A Thinking Fan's Guide to the Matrix Trilogy
   edited by Steve Couch

Sex and the Cynics: Talking About the Search for Love
   edited by Tony Watkins

Truth Wars: Talking About Tolerance
   edited by Tony Watkins

Spooked: Talking About the Supernatural
   edited by Tony Watkins

Playing God: Talking About Ethics in Medicine and Technology
   edited by Tony Watkins

Get More Like Jesus While Watching TV
   by Nick Pollard and Steve Couch

Teenagers: Why Do They Do That?
   by Nick Pollard

Saving Sex: Answers to Teenagers Questions About Relationships and Sex
  by Dr Trevor Stammers and Tim Doak

I Wish I Could Believe In Meaning
  by Peter S. Williams

If Only
  by Nick Pollard

Join Damaris and receive

discounts on other products from
Damaris and Damaris Publishing

access to web pages containing
up-to-date information about
popular culture

To find out about free membership of
Damaris go to **www.damaris.org**

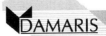